Other Men Will Come

How the Military-Industrial Complex Gained Control of the U.S. Government

Wolf Christoph Dieter

OTHER MEN WILL COME
How the Military-Industrial Complex Gained Control of the
U.S. Government

ISBN-13: 978-1503344723
ISBN-10: 150334472X

Library of Congress Control Number:2014921326
CreateSpace Independent Publishing Platform
North Charleston, South Carolina

Available at Amazon.com

Contacts:
wolfchristoph.dieter@yahoo.com
othermenwillcome@gmail.com
http://othermenwillcome.blogspot.com/

Printed in the United States of America

TABLE OF CONTENTS

Preface 1
Section 1: A Military Operation 7
Section 2: The Military-Industrial Complex and
    the Finance-Capital Group. 17
Section 3: Encirclement 27
Section 4: Containment 39
Section 5: Developing the Pax Americana. 55
Section 6: Overt and Covert Problem Solving 69
Section 7: Kennedy 81
Section 8: Military in the White House
    Truman to Carter 99
Section 9: Military in the White House
    Reagan to Obama 115
Section 10: The Weaponization of America 133
Section 11: War Without Soldiers. 157
Section 12: Other Men Will Come 173
Bibliography 191
Endnotes. 203

PREFACE

"The essence of war is deception."
Sun Tzu, The Art of War, 544–496 B.C.

We live in an age of great wars. Convulsive national wars began in the time of Napoleon Bonaparte and escalated over more than a century to international world wars and dozens of armed conflicts in and among nations. These conflicts have continued into the 21st century and will assuredly continue into the foreseeable future.

The Form of war and the corresponding world Form have changed with each generation. The history of wars between 1871 and 1914, the minutiae of that period, and its Form have been fully covered elsewhere. As such, this period is but summarized here. It was a time of growing mass armies, equivalent weapons development, and the staking out of the resources of the world for the culminating struggle that defined the great wars, the first of which finally began on July 28, 1914: World War I.[1] Germany and Austria-Hungary battled France, Russia, and England. A political assassination started it, but control of the rich resources of all of Europe were the true objective, not the untimely death of a minor player on the world stage. The United States reluctantly entered the conflict in 1917, bringing battlefield strategy, armaments, and men, which ended the war.

Nor are we concerned with the details of World War II. That war was the fulfillment, the peak of development of the military strategy and tactics that were used in World War I. World War II began on September 1, 1937[2] when Germany marched into her neighboring countries—all of which were resource rich—and was soon joined by Italy, after which Japan decided the time was perfect to launch its own battle for territory. Officers, soldiers, sailors, airmen, and their nations and peoples were caught up in the last of the international wars in which combatants faced and fought each other through the medium of mass armies and mass individualized slaughter. It will not happen again. Ultimately, 30 countries were involved in World War II. It is estimated that 17 million people died: 10 million in the military, and 7 million civilians. Another 20 million were wounded.[3]

It ended in 1945 after Germany was turned into rubble by conventional bombs and two major cities in Japan were flattened with one atomic bomb each.

In its aftermath, the United States has remained continuously at war for the ensuing 70 years. This prolonged period of war began for America on December 7, 1941 after Japan bombed Pearl Harbor. Since then, global war has never stopped, but has continued, demonstrating that we do indeed live in an age of contending states. Of issue, however, is the nature of war for the United States, for while battlefields are active externally on foreign soil, today, the most intense battle for America is the internal one between the military-industrial complex and the finance-capital group, world domination being the objective, the one to protect the soil of the homeland, the other to protect the global marketplace.

The battlefields America has engaged in abroad are aspects of *one* war that has included the Greek Civil War, Mao Zedong's takeover of China, the Korean-Vietnamese War, the Suez crisis, the Cuban revolution, the United States-Soviet missile crisis, the Nicaraguan Civil War, Iraq, Afghanistan, and the Middle East terrorist wars, all in their various manifestations.

One war.

The American objective in militantly participating in global conflict is to achieve a *Pax Americana* similar to the *Pax Romana* (Roman Peace) of the Roman Empire. Fight the enemy on its own soil and keep the homeland safe. The Romans achieved *Pax Romana*, which resulted in two centuries of peace at home and war abroad.[4] It was designed to be that way. Because a *Pax Americana* has been accomplished within the United States, questions naturally arise as to how it came to be and how much further it will travel down the Roman road to the finality of an *Imperium*.

The Roman military needed global reach within its known world because those areas represented sources of revenue for the wealthy of Rome. Similarly, the United States pursues oil availability to ensure the economy is sustained. The issue in the 21st century for the United States is not that terrorists might attack the country, but rather whether militant groups will be allowed to entrench themselves and develop an organized state in the Middle East. With money and the oil-rich resources of the area, militants could attack the European Union and England. If they stopped the shipment of oil, it would unbalance the economy of every nation on the planet.

This continuing war's exoteric manifestations have provided a subject for debates without the debaters realizing the central point, which is that, in addition to the obvious armed conflicts, a covert war has been and is being actively fought in the United States between the military-industrial complex and the finance-capital group. The object for both is world domination.

The military-industrial complex uses planned global war to ensure peace in the homeland. The finance-capital group engages in planned global war in the realm of financial markets to ensure the continuation of profits. Planned global war by the military-industrial complex is not necessarily a bad road for the West to travel in view of the sophistication of the weaponry she possesses in the epoch in which it is taking place. Planned global war by the finance-capital group is not about saving the United States from invasion and occupation; it is entirely about securing money for the 100 men who control two thirds of it in America.

These two forces are engaged in a grim, pitiless, no-quarter battle for supremacy.

Under today's conditions, a *Pax Americana* pursued by the military-industrial complex may well be the only way open to ensure the West's survival. From the end of World War II, it has been an age of war *par excellence*, all the more so the less it has been seen. There are those who will agree with this statement simplistically because of nuclear weapons: atomic, hydrogen, and neutron bombs. But concentrating on the brutality of those weapons, in effect bludgeons of world-destroying proportions, downplays the sophistication of the efforts being waged for worldwide domination by the military-industrial complex and the finance-capital group.

And we *will* wage wars, like it or not. We may regret it, we may lament it, but it is there. War is the *Zeitgeist*, the spirit of the age. War will not be legislated out of existence or go away. It is self-delusion to hope otherwise.

Section 1
A MILITARY OPERATION

*"A deep understanding of history is necessary . . .
not merely recent history which concerns with
the trivia surrounding conspicuous men and
events, but an understanding of that history which
records the main currents of the past activities
of men and which leads to an understanding of
what has created and what has destroyed great
civilizations."*
George C. Marshall, February 22, 1947

Before World War II, United States political policies served
the economic interests of the nation, and the governmental
response to foreign policy was geared to the requirements of
major business interests from banana republic intervention
to American involvement in World War I. This traditional
way of war was in place until the end of World War II.

After, it is another story.

Current interpretations ignore this fact and assume a continuity with the past that no longer exists. Delusive memoirs by key and often otherwise competent figures of the post-World War II era do not recognize the decisive difference and consequences of the historical period after World War II. No matter how much they may have studied the world, they miss the importance of the many armed interventions after World War II, which are different from those before because a grand design was conceived during World War II to alter the form of war the United States engaged in: the design for a *Pax Americana*.

President Franklin D. Roosevelt desired, in the postwar world after 1945, an American military *reduced to its pre-war size* with an estimated annual budget of about $5 billion a year.[5] Nothing could have been further from the desires of the industrialists who supplied the military with the weapons and materials for waging war or those members of Congress the industrialists were supporting. Contrarily, the bankers and financiers who dealt *not* with tangible goods, but instead with pure thought, the manifestation of which is money, were struggling for control of all money[6]. . . and our lifetimes.

The politicians around Roosevelt, and the president himself, never questioned their own power to cut the military. The industrialists and their military cohorts kept their own counsel even though such a disastrous cut in the military budget would have put the entire military back on the same ineffectual status from which it had arisen to win World War II.

It could not be allowed to happen.

The first labor pain of the Form of America in which we live today was the operation carried out during the Democratic political convention in Chicago, Illinois, in 1944.

World War II Americans lived (as they do today) in an operational world. *Operation* is used here in the sense of a military or intelligence operation. These operations can be as varied as the invasion of Italy and Europe by the Allies in World War II, a political assassination such as that of the Lebanese president in 1983, a military strike such as the bombing of Tripoli in 1986, a covert Central Intelligence Agency operation, a Navy Seal operation, or the Iran-Contra affair of 1987 that was organized under the umbrella of the National Security Agency.

The 1944 convention was an *operation*.

Operations are planned for specific objectives, after which techniques evolve to ensure the operation achieves the desired objectives. Effectively, the process is based strictly on facts and covert intelligence gathering, and ends with the application of sophisticated strategies to guarantee success.

In the Democratic presidential convention of 1944, no problems were anticipated for a fourth-term election of President Roosevelt. Part of Roosevelt's platform was *reduction of the military*.[7] If Roosevelt had his way, the military-industrial complex faced a massive reduction in size and importance. The convention's only real business outside the loud performance art of politics and the formality of Roosevelt's assured nomination was the business of nominating a vice president.

Henry Agard Wallace, former senator from Iowa and incumbent vice president, was considered an obvious winner. A Midwesterner was needed that year for the Midwest Democratic vote. Wallace was a humanist, a liberal, and even though there were those who felt he leaned too far that way . . . well . . . he'd make it anyway.

But there was another senator around, a senator with a record of strong military connections, one who had insisted the American military machine keep a clean bill of health and positive image during the war years while heading the Senate committee that monitored all military activities: Harry S. Truman of Missouri, head of World War II's famed Truman Committee that monitored military acquisitions.[8]

Truman went into the 1944 Democratic convention, and by whatever means, whatever backing, whatever operation mounted by the military-industrial complex, emerged the upset nominee for vice president of the United States.

The November elections that year brought him into office along with Franklin D. Roosevelt. Roosevelt kept Truman at a distance, in part because they had not arisen from the same social groups, and in part because Roosevelt wanted Wallace. The outcome of the election did not change things. Truman observed, commenting on his outsider's role, that "Roosevelt didn't even let me know about the developing of the atomic bomb. I found out about it only after I became president." [9]

Taking an operational view, the last half of 1944 looked like this:

1. World War II was ending. Only Japan was left to vanquish.
2. It was an election year.
3. As wartime president of outstanding popularity, Roosevelt would assuredly be re-elected and would continue in office through the decisive postwar years up to 1948, giving him plenty of time to carry out his proclaimed mission to reduce the military to prewar levels.
4. Roosevelt, though with some misgivings about the Soviets, anticipated his own leadership of the nation. This leadership included the marginal military budget noted earlier, which would leave the military unrecognizable from the mighty machine it had become.

Militarily, the problem was insoluble, in a civilian context. However, history's solution is . . . history.

Roosevelt and Truman won the election, but Roosevelt's fourth term as president of the United States was short-lived.[10] His last term began on January 20, 1945, when he and Truman were sworn into their respective offices. Three days later, on January 23, 1945, Roosevelt boarded the U.S. Navy heavy cruiser USS Quincy, which, with its escort vessels, left Newport News in the state of Virginia and steamed across the Atlantic and through the Mediterranean to the British island of Malta. From there, Roosevelt and his contingent flew to Saki airport in the Soviet Union and then motored to the Crimean port of Yalta, where meetings were held for more than a week between Stalin and Churchill, the

Soviet Union and British leaders, respectively. The subject of the meetings was the Form of the postwar world.[11]

Ten days later, the president left Yalta for Saki and from there, flew to Egypt to again get aboard the *USS Quincy*, which returned the American chief executive to the United States. He had been President of the United States and traveling for a little more than a month. Meantime, Truman was in Washington with no apparent duties or responsibilities.

A few weeks later, on March 29, 1945, Roosevelt left Washington on the presidential train for his famed retreat at Warm Springs, Georgia. He arrived the next day, the afternoon of March 13, and was driven to the Little White House at the springs.

For a week Roosevelt enjoyed the atmosphere of the resort, took rides in cars from the presidential motor pool, enjoyed the company of friends and relatives, sat for a portrait by an artist, Madame Elizabeth Shoumatoff (commissioned by his "friend" of 30 years, Lucy Rutherford, who was also there), held a press conference, and was looking forward to a barbecue with intimate friends scheduled for the afternoon of April 12.

Truman was out of sight in Washington, as was chief of staff of the U.S. Army, General George Catlett Marshall, a military man of quiet dignity who was a brilliant military strategist.

Late in the morning on April 12, Roosevelt was sitting for his portrait in the living room of the Little White House. Also present were his cousins, Laura "Polly" Delano and

Margaret Suckley, friend Lucy Rutherford, and the artist, Madame Shoumatoff. From time to time, aides entered and left the room on business. "The Boss" wore his Navy cape and read various papers and signed others.

About 1 p.m., he had a few spoonfuls of gruel, but no more. Moments later, he put a cigarette in his famous cigarette holder and started smoking. At 1:15 p.m., he put his hand to his forehead and complained, "I have a terrific headache" and collapsed.[12]

Those were his last words.

One of the Secret Service agents on duty stated later that the president collapsed, the Navy doctors arrived, then the military [security] came in and took over, and no one in the Secret Service ever saw him again. In the same moment a president is declared dead, the Secret Service turns to protect the next president. He was in Washington.

What has leaked through a tight security screen more than 59 years later is a chilling version of events. Within minutes, his valet, Arthur Prettyman, and houseboy, Joe Espencilla, lifted the stricken president from his chair and carried him into his bedroom. Military doctors, Lieutenant Commanders Bruenn and Fox, were summoned to tend to Roosevelt. Admiral McIntire, Roosevelt's personal physician, was phoned in Washington, and the admiral then called Doctor Paullin, a civilian specialist in Atlanta, and requested that he go the 70 miles to Warm Springs to attend to the president. It took Paullin close to 2 hours of driving to get there, the only civilian official to ever be at the scene. There was little for him to do.

He arrived at Roosevelt's bedroom just in time to be one of the three doctors to certify the president's death. The other two were from the military

It was 3:35 p.m. Central War Time on April 12, 1945.

Early that evening, a firm of Atlanta morticians was called in to arrange details. Also that evening came word that General George Marshall had assumed responsibility for taking care of all details of the event, including the transport back to Washington and the funeral.

There was no autopsy.

The gruel was never analyzed.

A team of civilian morticians from the Atlanta firm of H.M. Patterson and Son arrived before midnight with portable embalming equipment and proceeded to undertake the embalming of the body. After embalming, the question of an autopsy was moot.

Thus died Franklin D. Roosevelt.

It was a military operation from beginning to end.

Military men put him in a 600-pound bronzed casket on the morning of April 13 and took the body to the presidential funeral train at the station in Warm Springs. Over 2,000 uniformed troops guarded the procedure. At 11 a.m. Eastern War Time, the train left for Washington. The closed casket could be seen from outside the funeral train as it was pulled through various cities and towns on the way. An honor guard of troops guarded the entire route, from the state of Georgia to the nation's capital.

Twenty-four hours later, at 11 a.m. on April 14, the train arrived in Washington under heavy military guard.[13]

It was a military funeral. Roosevelt's casket was taken from the train by military pallbearers and put on a black caisson pulled by white horses. Hundreds of thousands of people filled the streets where the funeral column moved with its historical burden. The curbs were lined with troops at attention, a military guard every 6 feet along the entire route.

At the White House, the casket was placed on a bier in the East Room. Four sentries, one from each branch of the services, took their positions at the corners of the casket. At 4 p.m., a simple memorial service began in the East Room. It lasted half an hour. It was a closed casket service. The sealed casket was never opened after it left the Little White House in Warm Springs.

That evening, they put Roosevelt's casket back on the caisson for the return trip to Union Station. The funeral train started in the darkness of the night of April 14 for Roosevelt's ancestral home in New York state. The entire route of the train to Hyde Park, through Maryland, Delaware, Pennsylvania, and New York, was guarded by contingents of U.S. Army soldiers.

The next morning, at the estate in Hyde Park, the coffin was unloaded onto a hearse and taken to the rose garden at the family mansion. Military commanders, troops, Army pallbearers, and more than 600 West Point senior cadets attended as Roosevelt was put in the ground before noon on April 15, 1945.[14]

All but one subsequent burial of a president of the United States since that day has been controlled and conducted by the military.

With Roosevelt gone and Truman, the next president, in charge, the military budget was not reduced, and in fact, *it increased rapidly* and has never been significantly reduced since.

Ronald Reagan, on January 21, 1985, asserted, "There never has been a transfer of power by bayonet in America and, God willing, there never will be."[15]

No need for a bayonet when the mission can be accomplished with stealth.

In whose interest is it that four presidents of the United States since 1945 who have proposed reducing the size of the military have met an untimely departure from office through one means or another? One, Carter, who recommended a reduction in the military budget, only served one term and was replaced by a man who was the epitome of the military spirit: Reagan.

Proposing a reduction in the military budget is dangerous.

Section 2

THE MILITARY-INDUSTRIAL COMPLEX AND THE FINANCE-CAPITAL GROUP

"Would that the Roman People had but one neck!"
Emperor Caligula, 12–41 A.D.

In the philosophical sense, decisive currents of Form forge the world today. Some are political, others might well be called metaphysical. Some come forth fully into the light, while others can only be discerned through observation. Examples of the first, the political, are the Soviet Union, the Third World, and the West, with America as the *deus-ex-machina*. Examples of the second, the metaphysical, are America's "finance-capital group" and "military-industrial complex." These two warring factions are defined in this section. They are elemental currents decisive to the world and to we who live in it. They are prime phenomena—to use

Goethe's term—and key to our comprehension of America's decisions and acts, her moves that are so baffling to the non-Western world and to the majority of the West's population itself.

The military-industrial complex and the finance-capital group are in agreement as to an objective, but in fundamental opposition in their intrinsic world outlooks. Both strive for world domination, in democratic guise, for America. Each aims for itself to rule America, but for different reasons. Since World War II, the struggle between them, fought out in the banks and streets of the world's cities constitutes the real history of the age. The finance-capital group represents a form of money-thought, embracing the entire planet to the extent that if any one of the primary developed nations such as the United States, Germany, Russia, China, or England goes down economically, it will take every other nation on earth with it.

The origins of the these two warring factions started early in the nation's history when men set out to acquire as much wealth as they could one way or another. Those who became part of the military-industrial complex arose from the soil: farmers, rope makers, wagon makers, coal miners. They became the industrialists who built railroads, steel mills, ships, mines, automobiles, chemicals, pharmaceuticals, and armaments, among others. They acquired their wealth ruthlessly and with little regard to law or ethics. They dealt in the realm of things.[16]

On the other hand, the finance-capital group, as was brilliantly documented in Lundberg's *America's 60 Families*, including such men as Morgan, Rockefeller, Mellon, Du Pont, Astor, Goelet, Vanderbilt, Gould, and other extremely rich men, amassed their wealth through theft, bribery, fraud, intimidation, violation of laws, piracy, corruption, seizure of the public domain, extortion, larceny, and any other means necessary to make money.[17]

The men of both groups pursued money. They had no allegiance to ethics or to the consequences of their actions. For instance, the armaments industrialists sold weapons to both sides during the Civil War. They were driven by greed. The finance-capital group isolated themselves from those who dealt with things—the realm of things was anathema to them. Money is a form of pure thought; thus, a dollar bill has no value because it is just a piece of paper with some printing on it. Its value is assigned to it by the person who holds it and by the strength of the government that creates it. Money is the life's work of the capitalist. They have no use for anything else.

These two factions have engaged in ruthless combat for control of the destiny of the nation from the Civil War onward. Their selfishness is legion. The industrialists do not share their accumulated wealth with their workers; in fact, after importing slaves from Africa to use as cheap labor, they extended their treatment of slaves to all workers by paying them as little as possible, working them as long as possible, and establishing policies that would ensure the workers stayed workers just as slaves stayed slaves.

It is an attitude toward workers that prevails to this day. The money men are no different.

In the battle for money and control of the United States, which is the seat of their wealth and the future of it, these two groups of men have been adversaries from the beginning. Each created the methods and means of protecting their life's work from threats, both in the United States and abroad.

The industrialists funded a military capable of defeating any enemy through weapons, spying, and strategy, and developed a voracious appetite for the production of armaments, equipment, and supplies, and then made sure, by whatever means necessary, that the resulting machine of war would not become obsolete. The association of the industrialists and the military men came to constitute what was eventually termed a military-industrial complex.

And all in the name of "democracy."

But also in the name of democracy the money men enlisted rhetoric as their weapon of choice: the media. An arsenal of words and pictures was deployed as if it was guns and cannons to manage and mold public opinion. A bombardment of newspapers, articles, magazines, flyers, and radio broadcasts were used in the beginning to control the thoughts of people, turning citizens into a monstrous intellectual force intended to support the finance-capital group's aims—to make money.[18] Their arsenal today includes endless television broadcasts intended to produce impressions on the viewer, and those impressions support the aims of the finance-capital group; they influence the thought processes of the citizenry to take actions that benefit not the people, but the men of money.

Today, electronics are wielded like a battleaxe to capitalize on the actions of citizens whose opinions have been carefully molded to suit the finance-capital group's objectives. For instance, when a person tells a stock broker to buy shares of stock, in the space of the nanosecond between the transmission of the order to the stock exchange and the time when it is received, a powerful computer program intercepts the order. The program determines if the stock price is lower or higher by a point or two, and it automatically commands buy or sell, which retrieves a few pennies of profit. Multiplied millions of times a day, the pennies and fractions of pennies result in billions of dollars of profits, without any human making a decision.

The stock market and the men who control it can only make money when the market is volatile, going up and down, up and down, and they manipulate the circumstances that create that volatility through the use of the information media, which is comprised of propaganda. The news reports breathlessly announce that the markets are responding to fear of impending events, or optimism of anticipated good tidings, as if the markets were beings who could fear or hope. But the fear and hope are created by the news media, and produce the very volatility that brings wealth to a group of men so few a 3-year-old child could count them.

All in the name of democracy, of course.

But, alas, it is not a democracy when 60% of the wealth of the United States is owned by 1% of the population, and of that 1%, just 100 men own two thirds of it.[19]

And that describes an *oligarchy*,[20] not a democracy. Not even a republic, which the United States is supposed to be.

One of the offshoots of the need to protect and enhance wealth down through time has been the deliberate organization of an artificial aristocracy to make sure the wealth stays in the hands of the wealthy. In this country of immigrants who escaped from the divine right of kings, extremely wealthy men built vast estates, private schools, country clubs, yacht clubs, men's clubs, and other visible signs of astounding wealth to support a society to which only the rich could belong. They intended to be admired for what they had and not be remembered for the crimes they had committed to get what they had.

They lusted to be kings, so they created the outward illusion of being kings.

The descendants of these pretenders-to-be aristocracy have come to think of themselves as America's aristocracy, but in fact, they are nothing but the sons and daughters of a dazzling array of crooks.

To protect their wealth, these thieves did two things. First, they ensured that their sons and daughters would marry the sons and daughters of other wealthy men. That kept the money within a small group through intermarriage. They funded private universities, which were established as men-only educational institutions so their sons would learn how to manage money. They arranged debutante balls for their daughters so they would be presented to the other wealthy families as potential wives, all to keep the wealth within the select few. They created regattas and country club parties for the same reason, anything to ensure appropriate marriages.

And it worked.

Second, they bought relationships with politicians or organizations they needed to protect what they considered not only their wealth, but also what they considered "rights," which is how the Central Intelligence Agency,[21] the National Security Agency, and the biggest organization in the world in terms of how many people are employed—the Department of Defense—came to be. These organizations owe their existence to the richest men in the nation, and their primary mission is to protect that wealth and the means to make it bigger, to protect the divine rights of these new kings, at home and abroad.

To protect the oligarchy.

The productive economy (i.e., a factory, a farmer, a mine, and enterprises such as these) are rooted in the land under them. They are enterprises whose activities are merely indexed in money by the ebb and flow of it streaming through them in the course of their economic activity. The key here is that the *productive* economy is not free, not wholly able to move from that portion of the earth in which the constituent parts are rooted.

Only money is wholly free. The banks, the stock exchange, speculators, and raiders: the activities of these are free in that they can intervene in the activities of the economy for their own interests without the encumbrance of things. They can shift their resources with bewildering speed from day to day, hour to hour, moment to moment.

They are modern-day Vikings mounting their attacks on lumbering, immobile targets. Finance-capital's objective is not to creatively produce things, but rather to lay out their money in the form of invisible structures, to control even whole countries.[22] When finance-capital does lay out its money in this fashion, a side effect is that whole industries can be shifted globally for cheaper labor, cheaper products, with devastating consequences to the affected labor forces and market share organizations. This holds true with varying degrees of intensity for the entire West.

Along with Louis XIV, they could well have trumpeted (and some of them did):

"The State? I am the State."[23]

A few centuries ago, these providers of money were only a small part of the West's overall economy, supplying seed money for new productive enterprises and limited capital for the requirements of established business concerns. Finance-capital's overwhelming growth began with the Civil War and reached its peak with World War II. During that time, its members preempted for themselves, again in democratic guise, the entire machinery of the government of the United States, but their dominance did not survive World War II, for during World War II, the industrialists focused on controlling the means with which to ensure the survival of the nation. They also focused, concomitantly, on controlling the United States government. The fight was on.

The finance-capital group is not interested in the survival of the United States. They once were, in the beginning. But now their money is moveable, as never before, and it matters not in which country it finds a home. Their interests have shifted to the global marketplace, and the United States is just another pawn to be used in the acquisition of wealth. The only force holding the United States together and focused entirely on the survival of the nation is the military-industrial complex. Their singular focus is maintaining a secure nation. The well-being of the military-industrial complex depends on it.

Section 3
ENCIRCLEMENT

"Destiny? Policy is destiny."
Napoleon Bonaparte, 1769–1821

The military might of the United States was systematically demobilized and disarmed after each early major war: the Civil War, the War with Spain, and World War I. The finance-capital group made it happen. They saw no use in supporting a military in peacetime. It was expensive, and in terms of making money, a waste. Men in the legislative branches of the government who fancied themselves as better minds than professional soldiers, and in response to the finance-capital group, decimated the military, which in turn cost the industrialists their protection from decline and endangered their investments.

Before World War I, which occurred between 1914 and 1918, American military leaders, particularly in the U.S. Army, desired a more decisive say in United States foreign policy. During those many years the politicians in Washington had tinkered in military decisions, often with disastrous results. The effort to free the military from such interference was fostered behind a veil of secrecy by General "Black Jack" Pershing.

Pershing was born in Missouri in 1860 on a farm owned by his father, who was a businessman. He attended a private school exclusively for the children of wealthy parents and later attended West Point, not because he was fascinated by the military, but because it offered a better education than he could obtain in Missouri. He did well. He was praised by the superintendent upon graduation for leadership and acuity. His first battlefield action was against the Apache Indians in 1886, and he later fought the Sioux and the Cree tribes.[24]

In 1897, he became an instructor at West Point. From that date on, Pershing was geared for only one thing: war. He was disliked intensely at West Point because of his inflexibility. There, he was nicknamed "Black Jack," which was not a compliment. Major Pershing was then assigned to serve as an intelligence officer in the Philippines, where he met a young company commander many years his junior by the name of George Catlett Marshall.[25] Pershing was 37 years old and Marshall was 18 years old.

Sovereignty over the Philippines had fallen the year before to the United States after the Spanish-American War, and for years afterward, military missions were necessary to quell continuing disturbances in the islands whose primary population was composed of Muslim Moros. With little conscience and an abundance of disrespect for the indigenous people of the islands, in 1901, General Leonard Wood exterminated 600 men, women, and children who had taken refuge in a volcanic crater.[26] The result was years of military actions in the Philippines to keep control of a mutinous population. While in the Philippines, Pershing managed the battlefield conduct and conditions in campaigns against the Moros. He enjoyed it. Pershing quickly discovered that young Marshall was an invaluable strategist and they shared similar views of the Form of the military and its relationship to the forces that controlled the military in Washington. As their career trajectories diverged, they kept in touch.

Theodore Roosevelt, who was President from 1901 to 1909, liked Pershing immensely. He tried and failed to have him promoted to Colonel, and subsequently dispatched him on a diplomatic position to Japan, where Pershing learned the nuances of global politics. President Roosevelt, acting as Pershing's personal promoter, returned him to Washington after the Japan assignment and, knowing how to manage Washington politics, engineered a three-step skip in promotion for Pershing to the position of Major General. The year was 1905. Pershing was first based in Paris, France, spent time managing battlefields in the Balkans, and then was dispatched back to the Philippines.[27]

President Roosevelt then sent Pershing and a contingent of solders on an incursion into Mexico to capture Poncho Villa, a revolutionary who was threatening the southern flank of the country. The horse soldiers rode into Mexico singing a popular song, the first line of which was "Green grow the grasses, oh," which Poncho Villa's men heard as they hid in the nearby hills as "Gringo." To this day, Americans are Gringos.

The mission failed. Pershing had learned the hard way the value of careful intelligence gathering followed by sophisticated battlefield strategy. He also learned the value of developing a working relationship with the men of Washington who controlled his future, and he became good at it. In the end, Pershing, after all his different assignments, had accumulated experience and sophistication not just at managing battlefields, but also at managing politics.

World War I began in 1914 and engaged European nations in a deadly conflict against a German alliance focused on domination of nearby resource-rich nations.[28] The United States reluctantly and unwillingly entered World War I and only did so when it became clear that the economic interests of the nation might be compromised if Germany won. World War I had nothing to do with "freedom," nor did World War II. Wars in which the nation has engaged have been, 90% of the time, about money. For instance, freedom had nothing to do with the American Revolution, which was waged to ensure the economic interests of the citizenry against British greed, or the Civil War, which was waged to ensure that the South, which wanted to secede from the Union, remained economically bonded to the Union. World War I as well as the later World War II had nothing to do with freedom and everything to do with promoting and safeguarding the economic interests of the United States, and these wars were entirely in the interests of the finance-capital group.

It was a pattern that prevailed until the end of World War II.

The entrance of the United States into World War I was termed an "expeditionary force," not an "invasion," and Major General Pershing was appointed to take charge of the effort. He was joined immediately by Marshall, who was put in charge of training and operations as a strategist.

Military action in World War I by the United States up until that time had been met with sustained and energetic interference by both domestic and international politicians. Secretary of War Newton Baker, a friend and confidant of Pershing, was impatient with the constant interference in the disposition of the military by politicians in Washington, most of whom were pawns of the finance-capital group. As a result, Newton provided Pershing with unmatched power to run his military actions according to his own wishes. Pershing was given free rein to do what he wanted, order what military weapons and supplies he so desired, and fight the enemy according to his own designs. He did so with the able assistance of Marshall, whom he appointed as U.S. Army Chief of Staff. Marshall, in turn appointed Dwight D. Eisenhower as commanding general of the European theater of operations.

It was an appointment that would position Eisenhower to eventually run for president, and he owed it to Marshall. Eisenhower had come up through the ranks the hard way, with frequent checks on his advancement. But he was military to the bone, having become interested in war by reading his mother's history books. By trading working and schooling with one of his brothers, he eventually graduated from West Point, but not as a distinguished student. It was through experience that Eisenhower gained his prowess as well as his acquaintance along the way with military leaders such as Marshall and Patton, both of whom became prominent in America's victory during World War II.

At the end of World War I in 1918, a war that ended suddenly less than a year after Pershing and Marshall arrived with the American military, Pershing and other members of the military hierarchy undertook to achieve a more significant and permanent military force for the United States and to dethrone the finance-capital group from making further decisions about the conduct of war and support of the military. For indeed, the same men in Congress who chose to fund wars felt entitled to make battlefield decisions, often against the advice of the professional soldiers fighting the battles. The goal of the military, with the approval of the industrialists, was to ensure they alone would make all decisions pertinent to the aims and conduct of American military forces.

This goal was also the prime objective of two men of war at the end of World War I: Pershing and Marshall. They were in agreement that it was unconscionable that politicians in Washington with little or no battlefield experience and no practical knowledge of the intelligent use of weaponry and soldiers should be allowed to make strategic decisions about military matters. The friends of the military were the industrialists, ever interested in supporting any endeavor that would engage their resources.

Pershing began the effort to acquire control of the destiny and conduct of the military exclusively for the military-industrial complex with Marshall at his side.

At the end of World War I, Marshall, at the behest of Pershing, was appointed first to manage the training and planning of the First Infantry Division, and was then re-assigned in 1919 to headquarters, where he worked closely with the Pershing, who had become his close friend. It was a meeting of the minds formed on a global battlefield.

Marshall was born in Pennsylvania and, as the son of a prominent Virginia family, attended the Virginia Military Institute. After service in the Philippines under Pershing and re-assignment later to Pershing's personal staff, Marshall became the primary strategist of battlefield operations during the Meuse-Argonne offensive, which contributed to the defeat of the German army that ended World War I. His planning was surgical and precise. He and Pershing ran the war exactly the way they wanted and rebuffed efforts by denizens of Washington to change their battlefield tactics. The political elite had merely set a very generalized policy: win the war.

Having been given the freedom by President Theodore Roosevelt to control the war machine any way they so desired cemented Pershing and Marshall's decision to do something about the outside interference in military matters coming from the finance-capital group, whose aim was only to make and then protect their money, and not to defend the soil of the United States.

After World War I, Marshall was dispatched to various posts, both domestic and abroad, to teach mechanized warfare, disseminate information, and conduct training in the art of war. He became widely recognized as the most prominent scholar of military operations in America and, later, in the world. Enjoying a meteoric rise through the chain of command; he was promoted to brigadier general in 1936, just 3 years before Germany invaded Poland and began World War II.

Although England engaged Germany early in the growing war because of threats to their homeland, the United States political structure stalled any involvement. In 1938, Marshall, who was by then deputy chief of staff of the U.S. Army, openly opposed President Franklin D. Roosevelt when the latter proposed to send aircraft to England in support of English efforts to stop Germany. Marshall objected to the plan, the only person in the room to do so, on the grounds that it was precipitous as well as dangerous to engage America on the battlefield because of the lack of logistical support for the aircraft or training of the pilots.

Roosevelt listened carefully and then demurred. Instead of dispatching aircraft and untrained pilots with no supply chain to England, he appointed Marshall as army chief of staff. It was evident that it was only a matter of time before the United States would be dragged into the war because a German victory would have threatened the economic stability of the United States, freshly recovered from the Great Recession of 1930. Unemployment was still unacceptably high in 1938. Roosevelt commanded Marshall to organize and implement what became the largest military expansion in the nation's history. Marshall did so, increasing the military to four times its size within 3 years. War had not yet been declared.

In 1939, Roosevelt promised openly to keep the United States out of the war. The finance-capital group hesitated committing the media to support war or not support war, and their lack of decisiveness at this critical time was probably the most significant turning point in their loss of power over the military-industrial complex.

Roosevelt, at the same time, prepared the nation for military engagement by arranging for talks between United States military strategists and the British. He had Congress amend the American Neutrality Act so the Allies fighting Germany, Italy, and Japan could buy supplies from the United States. This action was promoted by the industrialists, who profited by supplying armaments overseas. The size of the U.S. Navy was increased, a salute to Roosevelt's service in that branch of the armed forces.

In 1939, Marshall's unprecedented fast rise to chief of staff of the U.S. Army was accomplished with the aid of Pershing and his influence with other military leaders, as well as a few politicians in Washington. Marshall was 59 years of age. It was the beginning of a new Form of war and clandestine control of the United States government by what was rapidly becoming the military-industrial complex.

Well into 1941, the American citizenry opposed any direct military involvement in the ongoing war. It has been speculated that Roosevelt knew in advance that the Japanese were going to attack Pearl Harbor and allowed it to happen to justify entering the war. Be that as it may, it would certainly serve the purposes of the military-industrial complex to allow circumstances to happen that would preclude abstaining any longer from entering the war. The best military strategist in the world, Marshall, had President Roosevelt's attention, but Roosevelt missed the hidden agenda, which was to support the industrialists and begin formation of a *Pax Americana*.

Roosevelt declared war against Japan.

Because Marshall was intimately involved in Pershing's machinations against the dominance of the finance-capital group, and the successes and mistakes thereof, Marshall had learned what approaches to the civilian political sector did not work, such as insistence that war was necessary to protect the mainland United States. It was better to point out the financial consequences if war was not waged, which attracted the attention of those congressmen backed by the finance-capital group. Better to suggest a limited engagement in terms of time and resources than an onslaught of withering military power. Better to speak of the military as servants of the House of Representatives and the Senate than to present it as the only thing standing in the way of defeat of the nation.

Marshall started his preparations to position the military-industrial complex to run the American government, when, as chief of staff in the early days of World War II, he was called back to active service in the Pentagon to head up a U.S. Army think tank charged with planning and implementation of the American military's role in relationship to the civilian sector in the postwar years. Marshall did not intend the military to be again caught with a naive trust in politicians to do the right thing, which would leave the military once again unprepared to fight a war, as it had been after World War I. As well, he had learned how efficient and effective the military could be without political control during his time with Pershing in World War I, when President Theodore Roosevelt granted Pershing permission the run the war any way he wished, at any cost.

The finance-capital group was always wary of the American military. For generations the American populace had been warned, through politicians, the media, and other means, of the very visible potential of the military to imperil American freedom, as opposed to the less obvious, but more real threat to freedom posed by the untrammeled economic and individual profit-making by the bankers and financiers. This skepticism and suspicion of the military reached to the highest circles of political leadership.

One example of these apprehensions occurred in World War II.

Within months of the bombing of Pearl Harbor, Marshall ordered creation of a school of military government in Charlottesville, Virginia. The purpose of this school was to train military personnel in the duties of government—according to Marshall. The declared objective was to train students for military government in nations that would later, hopefully, be occupied by American troops. This was undertaken in 1942, less than a year after America's entry into World War II.

The reaction of the civilian administration came shortly after. Marshall's official biographer quotes the general as saying, "There were accusations that we were trying to organize a new government" (at the school). At a meeting of President Franklin Roosevelt and his Cabinet[29] it had been rumored "that there was actually a plot to establish a new U.S. Government with a right wing political leader as President and Marshall as vice president." The discussions took up most of that day's cabinet meeting. There was well-publicized concern. The affair was resolved not long after when Marshall restructured his military government school.

The point here is that the matter was brought up for serious consideration at a meeting of the top American civilian leadership and demonstrates that the possibility of a military takeover was creditable to those selfsame leaders.

The democratic inclination of the general American population, up to and including the majority of the top administrative leadership, is of little importance in the colossal struggle between the two forces delineated here so long as the struggle was, and still is, in democratic guise.

It is not a matter of conspiracy.

It is a matter of the Form of the world we live in. It is the characteristic *style* of our era and the battle between a few score men (if indeed that many) whose destiny it is to be the leaders on each side, men of immense intellect and steel-hard natures, whose means, methods, and true objectives are little seen or comprehended by others.

Section 4
CONTAINMENT

*"The secret of all victory lies in the organization of
the non-obvious."*
Marcus Aurelius, 121–180 A.D.

Germany's leaders of the 1930s, eternal adolescents, created
a world of speeches, parades, and preening for the German
masses where they touted German superiority in front of the
world and German intent to conquer all, thereby organizing
and guaranteeing their own opposition worldwide.

They lost.

It was during and immediately after World War II that
the Western world witnessed the birth of the present era,
and more specifically, during the wartime administration of
President Franklin D. Roosevelt. The mercurial, manipulative
Roosevelt was the son of one of the oldest families in New
York, one of the so-called elite, a new so-called "aristocrat."
His grandfather acquired the family wealth through his

profitable trade with China in opium and tea and by real estate manipulations. Roosevelt grew up as part of the manufactured aristocracy of America and enjoyed a privileged lifestyle. He attended Groton School, where 90% of the students were from families on the social register of the very rich. Later, at Harvard University, he lived in a house populated by wealthy students so he would not be exposed to the common man.[30]

Ultimately, however, it was his personal philosophy, learned from the headmaster at Groton, that the working classes of America needed support if the nation was to survive long term, and a tightly controlled military budget, that brought about his suspicious death. During his presidency, he focused on programs of relief for the working man, recovery of an economy left staggering after a depression, and reform of ruthless Wall Street moneymakers. Most of his liberal programs came to naught after his death. Of all the programs that he instituted, only three remain: Social Security, the Federal Deposit Insurance Corporation, which protects those with little money from losing all of it when banks fail, and the Securities and Exchange Commission, which spectacularly failed to control the financial greed of the 1990s and early 2000s, which led to a deep recession starting in 2007 that primarily crippled the middle class. He was not a fan of the military.

But by far the most important figure in terms of the Zeitgeist, the spirit of the age after World War II and continuing today, was Marshall.

In the post-World War II world, Marshall was decisive in formulating the model for American military strength seen today and developed a strategic foreign policy, a policy under which the world has been living since World War II and which, today, is at its fruition.

Born in Pennsylvania in 1880, his father was a scion of an old and wealthy Virginia family. He graduated from the Virginia Military Academy and went on to become the U.S. Army's first five-star general and the only military officer to win a Nobel Peace Prize. The prize was awarded after he directed the development and execution of what came to be known as the Marshall Plan, which was intended to restore Europe financially after World War II, but was also the harbinger of his development of a *Pax Americana*: peace at home, war abroad.

Regarding Marshal's identification as a hero immediately after World War II ended, and preceding the execution of the Marshall Plan, was a period of deliberate starvation of the German people for 2 years by the withholding of food. The starvation was initiated by the U.S. Army under Marshall's command and was intended to destroy the strength of the German people, and it worked. In fact, it resulted in a massive black market that lasted until food was restored.

Nobel Peace Prize indeed!

Marshal was more than just a military strategist. He navigated his progress toward his goals brilliantly. For instance, when President Theodore Roosevelt put Pershing in charge of the conduct of World War II and Pershing recommended that his friend and protégé Marshall be put in charge of the European theater of war, Marshall, a resourceful commander, met frequently with Winston Churchill, who was the prime minister of England during the war. Amid all the accolades Marshall received following victory of the Allies in 1945, the most astute assessment of Marshall came from an observant Winston Churchill when he thoughtfully concluded that Marshall was "the greatest Roman of them all."[31] Churchill apparently recognized, in Marshall, a mind focused not just on winning World War II, but on an America after the war that would parallel the *Pax Romana* of the Roman Empire.

In the years after the war ended and before retirement, Marshall became chief of staff of the U.S. Army, a secretary of defense, and a secretary of state, and it was from those positions that the formation of a *Pax Americana* came into being under his guidance.

Marshall returned to the United States after Germany was defeated just as Roosevelt was in the process of being re-elected as President, a process he did not survive. Japan had yet to be defeated. After Japan surrendered, Marshall enjoyed the support of both the liberals and the conservatives. He greatly enjoyed the support of the industrialists, who stood to profit from the military machine that Marshall envisioned. He did not reveal his strategy for a *Pax Americana*. Congress subsequently supported his first objective, which was to begin the weaponization of the continental United States, which will be dealt with in a later section.

Marshall's relationship with President Franklin D. Roosevelt was never close. An anecdote is told that when they first met, the President unfortunately called him "George."

Once. But ever after, it was always "General Marshall" or "General."

As World War II was winding down, it could be anticipated that the two leaders, one military, one civilian, would become even more distant.

Also at a distance was a man named Harry S. Truman; in fact, he was practically unknown to Roosevelt. Roosevelt was astonished when, during the Democratic convention of 1944, this little-known senator named Truman beat out his preferred vice presidential candidate, Henry Wallace.

Truman had served in World War I in the U.S. Army as an artillery officer, and he became acquainted with Marshall at that time. To what extent Marshall engineered Truman's unexpected win as the presidential nominee is not known, but Marshall undoubtedly wanted a trusted military colleague in the executive branch instead of Henry Wallace if his *Pax Americana* was to become a reality. Wallace would have been the antithesis of what Marshall needed to support his vision. Wallace had a college degree in animal husbandry; he involved himself in agricultural interests and was known to possess bizarre religious beliefs, but worst of all, he had no military experience and agreed vociferously with Roosevelt that wars—all wars—should end.

He was anti-military. He had to go.

Roosevelt wished to refocus the nation from fighting a war to domestic issues. He made it clear during the reelection campaign that he wanted the military machine, so close to winning World War II at the time of the presidential campaign, to be quickly dismantled after victory so the money could be spent elsewhere. Roosevelt knew about the development of an atomic bomb, but neither did he approve of its use nor did he tell his vice president about it. After his surprise nomination and subsequent win as vice president, Truman was ignored. Truman was sneered at by the press as a "haberdasher" (a clothing salesman) from Kansas City, and then he was dismissed as just another in a long line of invisible vice presidents. Roosevelt considered him worthless.

On April 12, Roosevelt died and Truman was immediately sworn in as the new President of the United States.

Truman was informed of the atomic bomb.

He moved fast and decisively, Marshall at his side.

Less than 90 days after he became president, he ordered deployment of two atomic bombs to be loosed on Japan, the first on August 6, the second on August 9.

World War II ended less than a month later on September 2. To date, Truman is the only person who has ever ordered the use of an atomic weapon. The haberdasher, the seller of menswear who wore a little hat and looked dapper, had struck swiftly and with deadly force. Not long thereafter, he approved $13 billion for the Marshal Plan.

After Japan surrendered, the world of 1945 began with an overwhelmingly different configuration of power than had been the case less than 6 years before. There were only two major postwar powers: Russia and the United States.

Foreign nationals failed to recognize the change that had occurred in American government. General Walter Bedell Smith, former ambassador to Moscow, a close associate of Marshall and an early chief of the Central Intelligence

Agency, wrote a report about Soviet Politburo member Andrei Zhdanov's apparent summation of the world situation he had provided at an early postwar Cominform meeting.[32] Cominform, the Information Bureau of the Communist and Worker's Parties, was formed in 1947. It was established by Josef Stalin, Russia's leader, to address internal conflicts.

One question that was argued was whether or not to attend a conference in Paris to help organize Marshall's plan to reconstitute a devastated Europe. They decided against it on the basis that to become part of it would link them to the West economically, which might bring unwanted attention to their bankrupt finances. Besides, they had no interest in reconstructing Europe, they asserted when they refused to attend, a grave oversight in light of history.

Of interest here is the picture of the postwar world painted by Zhandov, spokesman for Cominform. Zhandov bragged that, as a result of the war, the West had *lost* three of its six major powers: Germany, Japan, and Italy. As well, the new "democracies" of eastern Europe had been transferred to the Soviet orbit. France had ceased to be a great power and Great Britain was greatly weakened. In addition, he contended, the peoples of the colonial and dependent countries were clamoring for liberation, and serious antagonism could be seen in the relations among the Western states themselves. It painted a picture of a world ripe for exploitation.

In fact, only the United States remained unchanged, and indeed, had been strengthened by the war, but Zhandov did not perceive it.

Also according to Zhandov, the Soviets and their satellites, the anti-imperialist camp, had enjoyed a great increase in strength. Zhandov concluded that postwar "New democracies had been recruited, the strength of communist and other anti-Western parties had grown enormously, and the strength of the Soviet Union made it more than ever a rallying point and "beacon of hope for all peoples."[33]

The Soviets had become a threat. They needed to be contained within their own borders.

The so-called Marshall Plan was a military strategy to stop Russia from expanding her territory to the west into Europe. Marshal recognized that an economically strong western Europe would present a formidable barrier to any effort by Russia to move into the resource-rich area. The Marshall Plan had little to do with "peace."

The second major step Marshall took to contain Russia was to trap the Soviets on their east, and it was taken in China. China had managed to forestall efforts by the Soviets to control the political processes of China, but two factions in China were struggling for ultimate control. The two factions were the Nationalists and the Communists. The country was on the verge of resuming a civil war that had existed since before World War II. It was to the advantage of the United States to ensure that China not become a close ally of the Soviet Union. In fact, a growing and strengthened China would inevitably endanger Russia and keep Russia occupied with maintaining their border with China. And it would keep Russian-sponsored Communism from engulfing China.

Goethe once declared, "To be a judge of history, you must have experienced history in your own life."[34] The quote is apropos of Marshall's background and the issue of China.

Marshall's initial experience in China was a 3 year tour of duty served there in the mid-1920s when he was 45 years of age, between the two world wars. He was no stranger to China's people or conditions. Chinese Communists were a blessing in disguise for Marshall's purposes. Experience had taught him that relying on the Chinese Nationalists for unification would be futile due to their corruption and the factionalism that developed out of the Chinese warlord system, which was continuing unabated. His assignment to settle matters in China concomitant with United States interests came about with Marshall's typical alacrity.

Marshall had turned over his office as chief of staff of the U.S. Army to General Dwight D. Eisenhower in 1945, then went home to retirement in Leesburg, Virginia, where, as he entered the house and greeted his wife, the phone rang. When Marshall answered, it was President Harry Truman on the line, asking him to go to China. "Yes," Marshall reportedly affirmed, and hung up the phone and that was that.[35]

It is often amusing the way key American epochs and decisions of the post-Roosevelt era are glossed over so lightly. Here we have a decisive step ("Yes.") taken by the most crucially instrumental man of this late period of Western civilization and it is treated anecdotally, as if reporting a phone-in take-out order to a local restaurant.

To pursue the matter further between Marshall and Truman, who was the tail and who the dog? Who wagged whom? Who or what created Truman's necessary vice-presidential nomination that positioned him to become president when Roosevelt unexpectedly died?

Marshall's China mission demonstrates the point.

It is not the focus of this treatise to go into the detailed mechanics of how Marshall's objectives were achieved in China or elsewhere. The purpose here is to state the overall objective of his postwar years and to present the major subordinate problems that arose, and then present the solutions that have reached their fruition today for the achievement of those objectives . . . which was and is nothing less than world dominion by America.

Marshall, in his sudden new role as Ambassador to China, spent a good deal of time during his 1946 negotiations in China with Chou En-Lai, the prescient, talented, Chinese Communist statesman, a key figure of later Chinese success in centralizing and organizing China, that is, industrializing for war purposes to the limits of the nation's capacity.

A Department of State history of Marshall's mission acknowledged that, "with some technical assistance from the War and State Departments, the new Ambassador to China [Marshall] virtually drew up his own instructions." And of interest, "Truman saw eye-to-eye [with Marshall] on the requirements of the mission."[36]

Marshall was 65 years old. Truman was 62 years old.

Then-Undersecretary of State Dean Acheson complained that Marshall designed his own ambassadorial chain-of-command by organizing communications in a manner that circumvented the Department of State hierarchy through which, as Ambassador to China, Marshall's reports would have normally and restrictively been channeled. In effect, Marshall established his own government within the government by substituting his own protocol.

The following incident occurred in the White House at a meeting between Marshall, Truman, and Dean Acheson, Truman's secretary of state, just before Marshall left for China in 1945. Acheson had served in the U.S. Navy Reserve during World War I and he was a lawyer. In Acheson's words, "Then occurred one of the important episodes of my life."[37]

"Mr. President," contended Marshall, "no sensible soldier undertakes a field command without leaving a rear echelon at headquarters. I would like to have one." He went on to explain that he would leave behind a representative who would receive communications from the field, get requests acted upon, and reply within 24 hours. This meant creating a highly placed representative."

"When [President Truman] asked how he wanted this arranged, Marshall pointed to me [Acheson]. I would be his rear echelon. He would use highly restricted military communications [the military had its own physical channels] and he would have an officer detailed to bring me his communications, at whatever hour of the day or night they arrived, and to assist me in getting them answered and executed. The President agreed enthusiastically, adding that I was to come to him at any hour for whatever I needed. The full significance of this arrangement was not slow in dawning on me. Here was, surely, a design for living dangerously...a special mission, with special communications outside those of the Department of State, reporting directly to the President through the second in command in the Department of State."[38]

[Later] . . . "we walked across the street to my office. The general asked whether I knew a suitable officer with whom I could work comfortably on his communications. I did. General John Hilldring, chief of G-5, in military government on the Army staff, had at his side an able aide, Colonel James A. Davis, a lawyer in civil life from Cedar Rapids, Iowa. He had earned my respect by outmaneuvering us in the past. I mentioned him, adding for its stimulating effect that General Hilldring would probably not let him go."

"I got him on the phone. General Marshall's end of the conversation went something like this: "Hilldring? General Marshall speaking. Do you have a Colonel James Davis? Very well. Have him detached and assigned to duty with Acheson at the State Department."

A dull crackling came from the receiver. "Did you say something, Hilldring? Tomorrow morning will do."[39]

That was how Marshall arranged it.

Marshall's instructions for his mission to China as ambassador were not from Truman, but instead were those he "virtually drew up" himself. They recommended "a cessation of hostilities be arranged [between warring factions] for the purpose of completing the return of all China to effective Chinese control" and, "develop an early solution . . . which will bring about the unification of China."[40]Marshall achieved this.

The unification was to turn China against Russia, not the United States.

China and Russia have been enemies ever since.

China was a tactical part of Marshall's overall global strategy. The purpose of his mission to China was to unite the country so that it would become a formidable power on the flank of Russia. As a land power and a mass-army power, China became a strategic threat only to Russia. Sophisticated weapons in sufficient quantity to threaten the United States were beyond the Chinese communists' capabilities for years to come, and by then the game was won.

China's ultimate threat to Russia, as envisioned by Marshall, was guaranteed by her 1945 population of 600 million, which was increasing at a rate of tens of millions a year. The threat of a mass population needing territory has come to pass. With a current population of 1.357 billion and still climbing, the only place China can go, in practical terms, is into the empty lands of the Soviet Union, with their vast spaces and enormous mineral wealth, or to the south and then east. Decades after Marshall's mission, millions of Chinese and Russian soldiers are occupied along their common border keeping each other in check.

Exiled Soviet writer Aleksandr Solzhenitsyn[41] anticipated that any Soviet war with China would last, "a minimum of 10 to 15 years and cost 60 million Russian lives at the very least." War with China, insofar as Russia is concerned, cannot be allowed to happen.

Russia was hence contained on the east by Europe and on the west by China, as was intended by Marshall's strategy. Russia was and is contained on the north by a geologic barrier known as the Barents, Kara, Laptov, East Siberian, and Chukchi seas, all of which are frozen, and beyond that the Arctic Ocean, also frozen.

That left Russia's border on the south.

The correct perspective on the Russian occupation of Afghanistan and subsequent so-called "peace" with a Russian puppet regime, which ultimately failed, was to perceive it as a defensive move not against American interests to contain communism, but against the potential of a Chinese move into the soft underbelly of the Soviet Union. The Chinese invasion and occupation of Tibet in 1962 was successful and opened a new source of revenue for China as well as room for population growth. Seventeen years later, in 1979, Russia invaded Afghanistan when the buildup of Chinese forces and population had engulfed Tibet and a new railroad capable of moving a mass army was headed from China to Tibet. China was on the move.

Thus it is that today Ukraine and Crimea are being herded back into Russia by Russia, a defensive move intended to barricade Russia against the Chinese, whose occupation of Tibet could have been interpreted as a warning of things to come. It also opened up better ports for Russian ships and, if the Ukraine government collapses, Russia will incorporate the breadbasket that is typical of the area, one that Russia needs because of a rapidly growing population. It is the only border Russia has that has any possibilities for expansion.

Marshall's machinations smoothing the way for Chinese unification under the Communists was a necessary part of the Marshall plan to land-lock Russia. It provided the basis for building strength on opposite sides of the Eurasian continent capable of keeping Russia within her borders: Europe on one side, China on the other.

Ukraine will fall.

Section 5
DEVELOPING THE PAX AMERICANA

*"Men will no longer see, nor understand, that
leader's work is the hard work, and that their own
life depends on its success."*
Dr. Oswald Spengler, The Decline of the West, 2013

Marshall's China mission ended with his return to Washington in December 1946. The next step was his nomination by Truman to become secretary of state, which was confirmed by the Senate on the same day, January 8, 1947. He was 67 years old.

The new secretary immediately set about reorganizing the State Department. A key figure in the reorganization was Dean Acheson, one of the continuing participants in the drama of the American World *Realpolitik* after World War II. At this juncture, he was still undersecretary of state and he revealed that he soon asked what Marshall expected of him. "I was to be his chief-of-staff [was Marshall's answer] and run the Department [of State], coming to him only when I needed help, and his look indicated that had better not be often. He wished matters needing his decisions to come to him through me and he would issue his instructions through me."[42]

On Marshall's arrival, the Department of State was a foreign office that actually looked primarily inward (rather than outward) to domestic issues of political and economic natures for its orientation. This seriously compromised foreign policy objectives and decisions, and was a heritage of the pre-World War II structure that had not changed appreciably since the turn of the century. During World War II, between 1940 and 1945, the Department of State had operated in a secondary role to the war effort due to the dominance of American military needs and objectives that controlled most facets of Washington politics.

The postwar Department of State was a hydra-headed monster subject to profound and divisive influences from political and economic interests, each with its own objectives in the major trends of American foreign policy. This meddling by diverse power groups was dealt with by Marshall quite simply. He established clear communication lines and a strong chain of command, as was his style.

The Secretary often betrayed his background by referring to the European theater. He referred to his associates by their last names, "Acheson" and "Kennan." When he spoke over the telephone it was always with a crisp "'General Marshall."43

Marshall in many ways as Secretary of State did not have to act much differently than as Chief of Staff during the war, for in 1947–48 there was [developing] a [new]kind of war in progress against Soviet Russia.[44]

In 1949, Marshall gave a speech at the Waldorf Astoria hotel in New York City in which he asserted that

"I found the problems [of America's foreign policy] from the viewpoint of geographical location and pressure to be almost identical in many respects with those of the war years. There was the same problem between East and West, the same limitations as to our capability, the same pressures at home and abroad in regard to various areas, and there was the same necessity for a very steady and determined stand in regard to these various problems."[45]

It was in this time that the phrase "cold war" came into currency.

Secretary Marshall's personal routine was not much different from what he had followed as chief of staff during the war, when he lived at Fort Myer and went back and forth to the Pentagon. He arrived at the State Department between 8:00 a.m. and 8:30 a.m. in his chauffeur-driven limousine from a downtown club where he lived. He returned to the club between 5:00 p.m. and 5:30 p.m. He was a military man on a military mission; it characterized his life.

By the time of Marshall's departure from office in 1949, the Department of State had assumed the quasi-military form that it has today.[46]

A significant demonstration of this form was the permissive "attitude" that accepted the role developed by the Central Intelligence Agency in State Department activities. In the field, the Agency can have as many people overseas as the State Department. In a number of American embassies, Central Intelligence Agency officers outnumber those from the Foreign Service in the political sections. Often the principal Central Intelligence Agency officer has been in the country longer than the Ambassador. The Central Intelligence Agency has greater funds to expend and can exert more influence than diplomatic colleagues.

In 1947, Germany was an occupied nation with a largely defiant population split in half between a coalition of western nations and the Soviet Union. Nations on the perimeter of the Soviet Union were in disarray and in no condition to participate in a world political struggle.[474849]The problem for the United States was to coalesce these elements, these nations, and align them to the American objective of containing Russia within her borders.

The first step was to demoralize the Germans, who had started two world wars in the space of 25 years. The second step was the 1947 financial donation of $1 billion U.S. and military support given to Greece and Turkey, a harbinger of financial aid that was to become the foundation of the Marshall Plan: the strengthening of certain countries to ensure a firm barrier against expansion by the Soviet Union. Thus fortified, Greece and Turkey were equipped to defend themselves against incursion by the Soviet Union and set the stage for them to join the European Union.

A declaration of American intent was provided in a speech given by President Truman to the U.S. Congress on March 12, 1947.

Marshall approved the President's speech in advance.[50][51]

Truman argued,

"Totalitarian regimes imposed upon free peoples [i.e., those not yet in the Soviet orbit], by direct or indirect aggression, undermine the security of the United States. I believe that it must be the policy of the United States to support peoples who are resisting subjugation by armed minorities or by outside pressures."[52]

The statement of policy, termed the Truman Doctrine, has been followed by the United States ever since, but was perverted by future president George W. Bush, as will be discussed later. A more sweeping objective was stated shortly thereafter in a speech Marshall gave at Harvard University on June 5, 1947. A key paragraph was his assertion that:

"It would be neither fitting nor efficacious for this [the American] government to undertake to draw up unilaterally a program designed to place Europe on its feet. This is the business of Europeans. The initiative ... must come from Europe. The role of this country should consist of friendly aid and support of such a program. The program should be a joint one agreed to by a number, if not all, European nations."[53]

The "friendly aid and support" opened the financial floodgates and the policy became a program of extensive expenditures with the amounts involved in multiple billions of dollars. It included Germany, the now-former bitter enemy. This latter policy was named the Marshall Plan and continued for years, with all those participating in the program on both sides of the Atlantic "winning." Europe got money and goods provided mainly, of course, by America.

Permanent air bases were established in several key nations such as France, Germany, Turkey, on Pacific islands, in Japan, and other locations far from America, but strategic to defending against aggression by Russia. The bases still exist 68 years after the end of World War II.

The Marshall Plan to create a *Pax Americana* was moving forward. Peace at home, war abroad.

In 1947, initial restructuring of the United States military by "enabling laws" laid the groundwork for a monolithic, but flexible, and overwhelmingly powerful American military-industrial complex. The 1947 policies for global domination created (a) a new Department of the Air Force, which, with the two old-line service departments of the Army and Navy, had their own secretary and undersecretary, (b) a new secretary of defense with "general direction and control" over armed services, (c) a new National Security Council, (d) the Central Intelligence Agency, and (d) other entities subject to the same central control. All this was the new "Department of Defense,"[54] which, for the next 3 years, embarked on a shakedown cruise by testing its ability to control governmental elements both domestic and global, expanding and, in some cases, removing inefficient parts of the new structure. Marshall managed it with an exquisite well thought-out strategy.

Marshall was at the same time closely connected to what was going on at the Department of Defense and covertly contributed to its reorganization while publicly keeping an official distance due to his position as Secretary of State. Meantime, he effectively, permanently, and factually established the Department of State as *subordinate* to the Department of Defense, a position from which the former has never been extricated.

By June 1950, the mechanics of reorganization and expansion were in place and ready for testing and growth. On June 25,1950, North Korea, backed by Russia, invaded South Korea. President Harry Truman, never one to waste time on trifles like Congressional approval, and backed by Marshall, declared war against North Korea 2 days later on July 27.[55]

On September 21, 1950, less than 60 days after the beginning of the war with Korea, Truman nominated a new secretary of defense, Marshall, who was confirmed on the same day. Marshall's tenure in this office oversaw the first wartime functioning of his recently created defense establishment.

At the time, although the departments of State and Defense were organizationally ready for war after Marshal had overseen their reorganization, the condition of military forces was not sufficient to support the notion that America could fight in Korea. Military hardware was antiquated, trained solders and the supply chains that support military missions were insufficient to fight a war, and citizens were in no way interested in the prospect of fighting another war so soon after World War II, no matter if it was described as "limited."

In the reality of the professional soldier's existence, human history is war history. On the world stage, those who renounce war subject themselves to those who do *not* renounce war. The only way to be in condition to fight wars *is to have wars to fight.* For the professional military leader, war provides a place to test soldiers and weapons, and in doing so creates a viable and veteran fighting force. It takes some years to turn a raw recruit into a professional fighting soldier, and this process is finalized *only* under combat conditions. To military leaders, a war is the only means to evaluate whether soldiers and weapons are battle-ready. For the United States, this need for a large fighting force in perpetual battle readiness became critical to maintaining peace at home in terms of Marshall's plans.

With the need of a good war to expand and test the reconstruction of both the Department of State and the Department of Defense, North Korea's invasion of South Korea on June 25, 1950, was a gift. Contrary to official disclaimers, it was *not* a surprise attack. The chief of the Central Intelligence Agency, in public statements and in private hearings weeks before it happened, had confirmed that the government was aware of the North Korean military buildup and the possibility of invasion.[56]

The question here is, to whose interest was it that such an invasion should occur, and at that time?

Statements and testimony by the then-Secretary of State Dean Acheson led some to dub the conflict "Acheson's War."

Acheson was an intellectual of some significance, but was also a former member of the National Guard, served active duty in the Naval Reserve, and was part of the group that assisted Marshall in organizing the Marshall Plan. Signals broadcast from Washington sources in the immediate pre-Korean War period included Acheson's publicized statements that defined America's Asian defense perimeter as including, Japan, Okinawa, and the Philippines, which "make the chain of defense absolutely necessary."[57] Note that Acheson did not include Korea or Formosa (currently known as Taiwan) in his "absolutely necessary" defense line.

Senator Tom Connelly of the State of Texas, chairman of the Senate Armed Services Committee, issued a position statement about the matter. In response to questions about whether the United States was considering abandoning South Korea, he answered that he was afraid it was going to happen whether we [the Americans] wanted it to or not because the Communists "can just overrun Korea just like she probably will overrun Formosa."[58]

Marshall chided Connelly with "Diplomatic action without the backing of military strength in the present world can only lead to appeasement."[59]

The Korean War and the Vietnam War were waged from 1950 to 1973. Both were actually one war, the same war, not different wars, and can properly be hyphenated, the Korean-Vietnamese War. It started slowly with token interventions and it lasted 23 years, from the North Korean march into South Korea in June 1950 to the withdrawal of American troops from Vietnam early in 1973.[60]

China is the key to clarification of the Korean-Vietnamese War and its importance in enhancing the power of the American military. In 1949, Chiang Kai-shek's army and the remnants of the Kuomintang retreated to their island stronghold of Formosa. After decades of war, Mao Zedong's forces finally ruled over all of China. Mao Zedong was the founding father of the People's Republic of China and he was a Communist. He immediately lowered a "bamboo curtain" around the new nation and proceeded to organize for bigger wars.

Initially, the Chinese were carried along by the momentum of their revolutionary fervor and ideology. They thought America was a "paper tiger" (Mao Zedong's term) and moved forward to get the United States out of the Far East. China took the American bait in 1950 by backing the North Koreans, who were immediately drawn into beginning the Korean-Vietnamese War. Their internal development and strengthening was fully in accord with Marshall's designs for a *Pax Americana*. A unified China presented an insurmountable barrier to Russia.

With the unification of China, an immediate requirement arose for the Americans to contain the nation on the south and east borders, where threats might arise against America's Pacific empire . . . and to make sure the direction of China's burgeoning strength was ultimately directed elsewhere towards the vast empty and inviting lands of Siberia and the Soviet Union.

The Korean-Vietnamese War gave America's premier military statesman, Marshall, one vital, active year of war before he retired to test the *Pax Americana* and permanently inscribe his mark on the Form, tradition, and pulse of years following and concomitantly set in stone the parameters that would perpetuate the most formidable war machine in world history: the Department of Defense.

With Marshall retired, Truman nominated Robert A. Lovett to take his place. By that time, the *Pax Americana* was a fully functioning phenomenon.

Lovett was a member of the finance-capital group. In spite of his several assignments in Washington government, he kept returning to his roots in banking and Wall Street between appointments. His father was chairman of the board of Union Pacific Railroad. He attended both Yale and Harvard and married a debutante. During World War I, he served in the United States and British air forces. He became acquainted with both Pershing and Marshall during that time.

In 1941, he became assistant secretary of war and, in that position, managed a massive expansion of the U.S. Army Air Force and later contributed to plans for intelligence services, which resulted in creation of the Central Intelligence Agency, after which he returned to Wall Street. Marshall called him back to be his undersecretary of state. By 1949, he had returned to Wall Street again. When Marshall became secretary of defense, he called him back yet again in 1950 as his deputy secretary of defense.[61]

Like Marshall, Lovett believed that the United States made grave mistakes when the government disarmed and weakened the military might of the United States at the end of wars. Thus it was that he was Marshall's hand-picked replacement to oversee the continuation of the military establishment so carefully crafted by Marshall. Lovett served that mission splendidly.

At the end of his tenure as Secretary of Defense, Lovett returned once again to Wall Street.

The Korean-Vietnamese War proved it is always essential to keep a world-class American military in a readiness condition. Korea settled any questions about the need for funding a fighting force and stifled any effective opposition in the Congress about the military budget. The Korean-Vietnamese War also ensured the updating and efficiency of America's armed forces in the only way it is ever possible: on the battlefield. Conveniently, the leaders of North Korea have generously timed their threats to invade South Korea about every 2 years, coincidentally the span of time between Congressional elections, which provides continuing incentive for the United States to maintain a vigorous American military presence in South Korea and train a rotating supply of soldiers for battlefield service. As well, North Korea has maintained a vigorous program of weapons development including nuclear capabilities.

What the Americans really accomplished has already been stated elsewhere,[62] but, quite simply, the North Korean incursion marked the beginning of an event welcomed by the American military and necessary at that time for its armed forces to arise, phoenix-like, from the remnant ashes of World War II and to further expand and train a military like no other that has ever existed in the world.

In the 2 years of the Korean part of the Korean-Vietnamese War, the military budget rose from $15 billion to $50 billion a year. By the end of the Korean part of the conflict in 1953, the military was well on the road to being refinanced, refurbished, revitalized, and in control of America's future. The next step in its growth was the war in Vietnam.

Politically, the war in Vietnam was the same as the war in Korea: to contain Russia. They were the same war. Two other reasons for moving a military presence into Vietnam were first, to further harden the fighting prowess of American forces, and second, to develop and test weapons of overwhelming effect and the mechanics of moving a fighting force anywhere in the world.

Military aid to Vietnam had already begun in a substantial way before the conflict in Korea was winding down. By the end of the Korean conflict in 1952, more than 200 American supply ships had already unloaded their military cargos in Saigon, Vietnam. Also, the nature of war was changing from the mass armies that had held sway for almost a century[63] to smaller more devastating units, Green Berets, Airborne Rangers, and Navy Seals, front soldiers of the new era with matching armaments, weaponry, and intelligence gathering. By using volunteers to populate the armed forces and raising the standards for acceptance, the United States now had the smartest, most dedicated, fiercest elite soldiers in the world.

Section 6
OVERT AND COVERT PROBLEM SOLVING

All we see before us passing
Sign and symbol is alone;
Here, what thought could never reach to
Is by semblances made known . . . .
                    Goethe's *Faust*, Part 2, Scene 5

The military-industrial complex presents the world with their own version of events that have to be dealt with: a case in point, the Korean-Vietnamese War. Based on results, Marshall's primary objective in 1950 was refurbishing the military establishment to the high-efficiency and war-keen capabilities it had in World War II, only with improvements, a prerequisite to the needs of his envisioned *Pax Americana* and domination of American foreign policy.

Marshall's tactical work of the day during this time became the limiting of the war to objectives he considered feasible and best for the United States' overall interests. Marshall ran the Korean-Vietnamese War as he had America's war effort in Europe in World War II. The importance of his activities as secretary of defense in the Korean-Vietnamese War fine-tuned his creation of the Department of Defense under the living conditions of an actual war.

His immediate strategic priority was personnel: the continuing selection and assignment of his own elite in the military officer corps from his supreme position as secretary of defense, they were meant to carry on his work in the coming years . . . but first, there was the problem of some chaff to be eliminated.

What happened in the case of General Douglas MacArthur provides an example that gives insight into the *actual* objectives of the Korean-Vietnamese War, a long-term policy of military-industrial objectives, and overt and covert operations. MacArthur became an overt operation.

General Douglas MacArthur was not a member of the handful of those conversant with the objectives of the new military-industrial complex designed by Marshall. MacArthur, a creature of the late 19th and early 20th Century, was fully in command of the techniques of mass army and amphibious operations of his era. And of his own publicity. He was a five-star general and supreme commander of allied forces in Europe during World War II. Later, he became supreme commander of the southwest Pacific area. He was appointed to manage the occupation of Japan, and led the United Nations command early in the Korean-Vietnamese War.[64]

In December of 1950, the presence of a large number of Chinese soldiers was detected in northern Korea; they were integrating with North Korea's army.[65] MacArthur had higher personal political aims than to be simply a successful field commander of the Korean-Vietnamese War. He envisioned a smashing victory over North Korea and the rich rewards it would bring to his persona, a persona that also envisioned becoming a future president of the United States. Hence, he intended to move to interdict the Yalu River bridges and, from there, proceed with a vastly expanded war that could well serve his own objectives and ambitions. The Yalu River is on the border between North Korea and China. Marching an army to the Yalu would have engaged America in a land war with mainland China. European leaders expressed fear of a major war with China and the possibility of the use of more nuclear weapons by the United States.

MacArthur had to be stopped.

A land war with China was contrary to Marshall's long term goals.[6667] MacArthur was relieved of command and dismissed from office concomitant with a recommendation made by Secretary of Defense Marshall to the man who did the firing, Harry Truman. Marshall wrote the actual dismissal order himself.

MacArthur later grumbled that it did not matter who the firing squad was, that Marshall had pulled the trigger.

MacArthur had played for high stakes and lost.

Marshall's term as Secretary of Defense, which ended with his retirement in 1951, was the finale of Marshall's high profile years and brought his creation, the *Pax Americana*, into being. After retirement, he disappeared behind a veil of secrecy. His work was done.

Of note was a comment made by Arthur Schlesinger, Jr.

Schlesinger was one of the nation's foremost commentators on the state of the nation. Unable to pass the military medical examination for service in World War II, Schlesinger was employed by the Office of War Information as an intelligence analyst for the Office of Strategic Services, from which the Central Intelligence Agency arose. Based on his experience, Schlesinger stated that, by the 1950s, the Central Intelligence Agency had acquired a power that blocked State Department control over the conduct of foreign affairs. In fact, Marshall had organized the most effective covert operations organization in the world 50 years before it came to the attention of either the Congress or the public. They had already been operating at full efficiency well before the war in Vietnam.

The official Department of State account of Marshall's tenure as secretary of state contains the following assessments: "Truman worshiped Marshall." Some things the president said about Marshall are also quoted: "The most remarkable man I ever met." "One of the great men of this age." "The greatest living American." "[I] . . . can always count on Marshall."[6869]

Truman was asked to name the person he thought had made the greatest contribution to the state of world affairs in the preceding 30 years and he immediately named

Marshall. Truman observed, "I don't think in this age in which I have lived that there has been a man who has been a greater administrator, a man with knowledge of military affairs equal to General Marshall."

Eventually, sealed archives will become available detailing his long-term strategic activities during his career in structuring and giving form to the defense hierarchy and creating the foundation upon which the nation enjoys peace at home and fights wars elsewhere. The task of knowing the technical specifics about his activities must be left for the future, when the resource materials are no longer under security measures. But for now, we can see his results, and from those derive some insight into his motives and ultimate aims.

The *Pax Americana* he created has since become a self-sustaining phenomenon, as will be shown.

Marshall's legacy by then in place and secure, the chronology[70] of the Korean-Vietnamese War illustrates the unfolding of his design that provided the first test of the military-industrial complex in control of the United States government. In 1951, the United States entered into a mutual defense agreement with France, Vietnam, Cambodia, and Laos for *indirect* United States military aid to the latter three. This was 2 years *after* Marshall ordered the armed forces to begin sending supplies to Vietnam.

As early as 1949, Marshall, as Secretary of Defense, had been shipping military equipment and support supplies to Vietnam. By October 1952, before the Korean-Vietnamese War was supposed to come to an end when an armistice was arranged, as was noted earlier, a large fleet of ships had already arrived in South Vietnam carrying military supplies bound for use by Americans. Marshall and Truman knew exactly what was going to happen next and had begun preparing for it well before the Korean conflict came to an uneasy stalemate, punctuated with North Korean threats and its continual preparations for all-out war.

The two wars were, therefore, one war, with one purpose.

The Korean-Vietnamese War had strengthened the United States military and the fighting force was in the process of being shifted to South Vietnam to create the need for an expansion of the military budget. The announced purpose was to ensure "freedom" of the people and ensure a democratic process of government, as opposed to Communism. The unannounced purpose was the same as behind the war in Korea: to establish a line beyond which the Soviet Union could not expand into land mass on her southern flank.

On the home front, in 1953, former General Dwight D. Eisenhower replaced Truman as President of the United States. Appointed by Marshall during World War II as supreme commander of allied forces, Marshall and Eisenhower had made many military decisions together. Eisenhower pursued Marshall objectives. He promptly threatened North Korea with nuclear intervention, which brought the war to a close in the same year.

War on another front, South Vietnam, was already well under way. It takes time and carefully planned logistics to move an army, air force, and navy, and Marshall left office as Secretary of Defense with that movement well under way in South Vietnam.

In 1954, Eisenhower, in a letter to the South Vietnamese president, remarked that American assistance would be given directly to the government of South Vietnam . . . but direct aid was already pouring into South Vietnam and armed intervention had been under way covertly in Cambodia and Laos for some time, directed by the Central Intelligence Agency and utilizing military assets. A year later, the full fighting force of the United States was openly engaged in North and South Vietnam.

Visible military operations were not the only intervention. There were *complications* in the leadership of South Vietnam that could have curtailed a military operation in the country, which was the next move in the testing period of the *Pax Americana*. Those complications had to be dealt with.

Covert operations were organized to ensure no interference forestalled the movement of the United States armed forces into South Vietnam. An example is to be found with the demise of the leader of the country, Ngo Dinh Diem, who was a *complication*.

When Diem became Premier of South Vietnam in June 1954, few thought he would last long in the job, not even a year. But he did, and spent most of the next 9 years establishing and consolidating his power in the chaos of South Vietnam politics.[71]

Within the first 2 years, Diem had, by national referendum, changed the form of government to a "republic" with himself as president with full plenary powers. The war raged on while America continually escalated military involvement with concomitant increases in the military budget back in Washington. In the United States, the Eisenhower administration came to an end in 1961 with the election of John F. Kennedy.

The United States had been in continual war for 11 years when Kennedy took over.

By the spring of 1963, President Ngo Diem's governmental organization provided him with the basis for negotiating a political, not a military, settlement with the North.[72] Diem especially wanted the Americans out. He was suspicious of their motives and thought they were "a political liability and a potential threat."[73]

In May 1963, his brother, Nhu, stated that Diem wanted half the American military personnel to leave the country as soon as possible. But reducing the military presence in South Vietnam was not on the agenda of Eisenhower. The military budget in Washington was growing rapidly and the military-industrial complex was fully engaged in a process intended to result in control of the United States government . . . and world domination.

At the same time that Diem and his brother were threatening to reduce the United States military establishment in South Vietnam, Nhu put out feelers to negotiate a peaceful settlement with North Vietnam. He undertook the initiation of discussions by having the chief of the Polish delegation of the International Control Commission, Mieczyslaw Manbeli, make the first overtures for a peaceful settlement through French Ambassador Roger

Lalouette. Any such communications were well known to the United States because of sophisticated covert operations that had been deployed long before.

The North Vietnamese in Hanoi responded positively to these overtures and were all for negotiating a settlement that would include

1. a cease fire,
2. United States forces leaving South Vietnam (there were only 12,000 to 13,000 in the country at that time),[74] and
3. creation of a limited coalition government that would keep the Hanoi and Saigon governments separate for some years and only very slowly permit their coalescence into one nation.

These proposals were aimed at protecting the south from being overwhelmed by strong-arm tactics from the north. The negotiations were scheduled to be completed with a definitive agreement between the parties, and both Hanoi and Saigon scheduled representatives to meet for this purpose in a neutral nation, India, in November 1963.[75]

Peace would have reduced or eliminated American military forces in the country.

But the question here is to what degree do the powers that rule America resort to assassination to achieve their objectives?

South Vietnam and the fate of Ngo Dinh Diem offers an illustrative configuration of circumstances that answer this question.

In 1963, a negotiated peace with North Vietnam or the complete pullout of United States forces from the country would have been disastrous to the United States military.[76] In November 1962, rebel troops in Saigon, aiming at the removal of President Diem, threw up road blocks at key points throughout the city, took over police headquarters, communications centers, Navy headquarters, and surrounded the presidential palace. It was never made clear what fomented these precise actions. Fighting broke out between the rebels and military forces loyal to Diem and lasted through the afternoon and into the evening.

The palace was encircled by rebel troops when, in the darkness of night, Diem and his Brother Nhu left secretly through a tunnel that led into the woods outside the palace grounds. They were met by a car that took them into Cholon, the Chinese district of Saigon. The fighting continued after they had gone, as none of the troops involved knew they had left.

Diem and Nhu stayed overnight in the home of a loyal Chinese merchant. They left the house early to seek sanctuary in the church of St. Francis Xavier.

Somehow, the rebels found out where they were. To whose advantage was it that their hiding place be found?

Just before 10 a.m., three armored cars from the rebel forces arrived and cut off the church from outside contact. They were under the command of General Mai Huu Xuan. The brothers were enticed out of the church, seized, their hands tied behind their backs, and they were shoved into one of the armored cars commanded by Major Nguyen Van Nhung, an aide to rebel General Duong van Minh.

The three vehicles started back to general staff headquarters. On the way, Major Nguyen seized his bayonet and repeatedly stabbed Nhu until he collapsed, dying, on the floor. Then the major took out his pistol, shot Diem in the head, and after, for good measure, put a bullet through Nhu's brain.[77]

The *complication* ended.

How many more such strategic deaths have been the result of well-planned military operations over the years?

From there, the fighting escalated and then went on for years, the only major war in the world at the time. Millions were involved around the globe, hundreds of thousands in North and South Vietnam, and the whole of America was convulsed for years in the throes of the conflagration. The cost of the Korean-Vietnamese war in American dead was over 50,000 in Korea by the time of the 1953 truce, and another 60,000 in Vietnam had expired by the time of the 1973 cease fire and America's departure from South Vietnam.

The corresponding figures for the wounded Americans were close to 100,000 in Korea and 150,000 in Vietnam—the Korean-Vietnamese War was consequently less deadly than World War II. The conflict resulted in protests by anti-war activists in the United States, led with vigor by the media under the guidance of the finance-capital group, which resulted in two actions. First, the onslaught of anti-war propaganda resulted in the appalling and shameless abuse of returning veterans. Second, anti-war sentiments supported the ambitions of the finance-capital group because that war, any war, would and did interfere with making money.

As a curious note in history, President Dwight D. Eisenhower was extensively involved with the military-industrial complex during his two terms in office. Perhaps not fully understanding the control it had over the affairs of the United States government when he took office, or that Marshall was behind it, it was he who named the phenomenon after dealing with it for 8 years. Convinced that it was bigger and more powerful than the office he occupied, in his closing political statement in 1961, as he left office, he warned the country to beware of the "military-industrial complex."[78] It was he who coined the term well after it had become a reality. He warned,

"An immense military establishment and large arms industry [are] new in the American experience. The total influence—economic, political, even spiritual—is felt in every city, every statehouse, every office of the federal government. We recognize the imperative need for this development. Yet we must not fail to comprehend its grave implications. Our toil, resources and livelihood are all involved; so is the very structure of our society. In the councils of government, we must guard against the acquisition of unwarranted influence by the military-industrial complex. The potential for the disastrous rise of misplaced power exists and will persist. We must never let the weight of this combination endanger our liberties or democratic processes."[79]

It was a statement by one who denied his own heritage in the military, but by then, it did not matter, for it was already too late.

Section 7
KENNEDY

*"All governments were ready to repudiate the
individual spy -- if caught."*
Richard Rowan, Spies and the Next War

In the passage of history, it has become dangerous for any leader, foreign or domestic, to suggest interfering with the aims of America's military-industrial complex or to threaten the nation in any manner.

The material result for America after the Korean-Vietnamese War, aside from the success of the long-term China policy, was that the nation now had the most experienced body of officers, noncommissioned officers, and troops of any of the world's powers and a tempered number of military leaders winnowed out by a generation of war and combat. On the home front, a rejuvenated and unparalleled military hierarchy directed all this and, in the arena of *Realpolitik*, dominated the nation's life. But another *complication* developed.

John F. Kennedy, youngest elected president in American history, was a product of the finance-capital group.[80] The key to Kennedy, in fact, to all the Kennedys, is to be found in the father, Joseph P. Kennedy, and in the way he saw the world, dealt with the world, and in the way he raised his close-knit family and passed on to them his own heritage and style.

Kennedy senior had no qualms about his career as a money maker or of his blue-ribbon membership in the money (not social) classes of America. Twenty years after his 1912 graduation from America's noted Harvard University during the Great Depression of the 1930s, Joseph P. Kennedy was asked, as part of a follow-up report on his graduating class, what his profession was. His answer that he was a "capitalist" was an absolutely accurate statement.[81]

The elder Kennedy was the epitome of the free-roving, lone capitalist making deals of any sort that would make him a profit. He raided like a Viking, struck his deals sharply, often where least expected, and piled up his wealth. His was an economic dynamo.

He went from comparatively limited and humble circumstances in his childhood to become one of the wealthiest individuals in the country. By the mid-1950s, *Fortune* magazine rated Joseph P. Kennedy the 12th richest man in America.[82]

He raised his family to win. Second place was not good enough. Within the family, this often led to terrible sibling rivalries with lifelong effects. But winning was all that mattered. The German language has a word for this kind of activity, and had the Kennedy family been German instead of Irish, the motto for a family crest could appropriately have been *Totseigen*, which translates as "winning oneself to death."[83]

Disputes and the order of rank within the household were settled by the father when he chose to. The elder Kennedy operated the family on an internal seniority system. First in line was the oldest son, Joseph P. Kennedy, Junior.

Before World War II, Joseph P. Senior had the United States presidency as an ultimate objective for Joseph P. Junior, his first son. It was the son's inculcated ambition to become the first American Catholic president. But on August 12, 1944, 29-year-old Joseph P. Junior, at that time an American Air Force lieutenant, took off from an English airfield with a copilot on an experimental bombing run to the European continent. The plane was stuffed with explosives. The men were to pick a target, set the autopilot to hit it, and bail out. Shortly after takeoff, the aircraft blew up with such a tremendous explosion that no trace of the plane's occupants was ever found.[84]

The heir apparent, the next son in line, John F. Kennedy, stepped into his dead brother's shoes. The ceremonial declaration of this fact was made in Hyannisport in September 1945 by his grandfather, John F. Fitzgerald ("Honey Fitz") Kennedy, former Boston mayor and three-term U.S. Congressman, who proposed the following toast at a family reunion: "To the future president of the United States, my grandson, John Fitzgerald Kennedy."[85] Young Kennedy was handsome, charismatic, quick-witted, and clever with words.

The first step to fulfilling this hubristic toast was to get the young scion elected to his first public office. The opportunity arose the next year, when a seat in the U.S. House of Representatives opened up in East Boston in the 11th district.[86] In that first election, the young Kennedy won over his opponent with an overwhelming vote.

Kennedy's father, Joseph P. Kennedy, was the organizer of the campaign. He controlled the purse strings and was more than willing to spend whatever it took. His intention was "to sell Jack like soap flakes" [with] "the most elaborate advertising effort ever seen in a Massachusetts Congressional election."[87] The resulting campaign was sophisticated and effective.

It set the pattern for future Kennedy elections on the way to the White House as well as other candidates in the future who chose to use the Kennedy organization in pursuit of political office.

Kennedy went from that first election win to many others, as follows:

Elected to the U.S. House of Representatives.

Re-elected to the House.

Re-elected to the House.

Elected to the U.S. Senate.

Re-elected to the U.S. Senate. Two years later, he was in position to run for President of the United States.

In 1960, the Democratic Party was home to both Lyndon B. Johnson and John F. Kennedy, opposites in the battle between the military-industrial complex (Johnson) and the finance-capital group (Kennedy). Both were candidates for their party's nomination for the United States presidency.

The Democratic National Convention was held in Los Angeles in the State of California. The Kennedys were there, scattered in various homes and hotels around the city. Joseph P. Kennedy, the now-patriarch and John's father, was in nearby Beverly Hills in the mansion of Marion Davies, long-time mistress of nationwide newspaper publisher William Randolph Hearst. The two men were part of the finance-capital group to the core. The senior Kennedy worked behind the scenes and on the telephone, exercising his power and influence over those who could manage votes for his son to get the nomination.[88] John circulated among the delegates.

The two points of view between candidates Johnson and Kennedy were defined by media under the control of the finance-capital group, then and now the manner in which the media shape public opinion, especially when political battles are afoot.

The days of the Korean-Vietnamese War were the last hurrah for the traditional instruments of the finance-capital group for creating public opinion: newspapers and print media. Today, a plethora of electronic media has been added to the arsenal of the finance-capital group, which, as ever, uses it to influence what people believe. Their ammunition is words; their object is to beguile the public into believing a specific point of view to accomplish one of their own goals: money.

Lyndon B. Johnson had begun his official political career in 1937, when he won an election contest for a seat in the House of Representatives upon the death of one of its members. Johnson represented the State of Texas. He was a big, imposing, roughneck of a man, and as such he had the opposite public presence of Kennedy, who was handsome, charismatic, and well-spoken. Johnson was a military advocate as a matter of pride.

From his first days in Washington, Johnson had cultivated close ties with the United States military.

His first committee appointment was to the House Naval Affairs Committee in 1937. He remained on this committee as long as he was a member of the House of Representatives.[89] During World War II, he became chairman of a five-man subcommittee of the Naval Affairs Committee charged with investigating the Navy procurement program and the Navy's management of sea warfare.[90] For those matters, his subcommittee, in its purview, became a miniature equivalent of Truman's Senate committee working on upgrading the military. In the closing days of World War II, he had become a member of the House Committee on Post-War Military Policy. His advocacy was for a policy that would ensure that America be kept militarily strong with effective, far-flung military bases and extensive military manufacturing facilities.[91]

He was elected to the Senate and remained there from 1949 to 1961, 6 years of which were spent as a very powerful Senate majority leader. Johnson, though on a lesser scale than Truman, undertook a one-man campaign against military incompetence, inefficiency, and waste, particularly in the matter of expediting the delivery of military supplies to the global fighting fronts, and in these efforts, he had the full cooperation and support of the top strategist of the American military hierarchy: Marshall. They were mutually appreciative of each other.

Johnson became the Democratic leader of the Senate in 1953 and was elected to a second term in 1954.

He lived a political life committed to the military.

And he was on a collision course with a member of the finance-capital group: John F. Kennedy.

In the background, it had become dangerous for any leader, foreign or domestic, to suggest interfering with the aims of America's military-industrial complex. A rejuvenated and unparalleled military hierarchy was strong and determined, in the arena of *Realpolitik*, to dominate the nation's life and stay in control of any situation—globally. The United States was more than ready for the next war. And Johnson was its champion.

Johnson's supporters set themselves up for the infighting of the convention nomination for president. The Kennedy forces fought the Johnson supporters as they had for months, with a characteristic driving ruthlessness and effective organization they always demonstrated in the electoral process, and it resulted in the early victory of Kennedy on the first ballot: Kennedy: 806, Johnson: 409.[92]

With the victory of their candidate, many of Kennedy's backers and supporters were overjoyed to finally be done, once and for all, with the tall provincial-looking Texan, and most thought they had seen the last of him.

However, to their consternation, the following morning, the new presidential candidate Kennedy offered the vice-presidential spot to Johnson. He felt it was a generous gesture to keep peace in the party and well knew that he could isolate Johnson to near obscurity if he became vice president.

Johnson accepted the offer and did not explain then, or ever after, why he had been willing to trade being the second most powerful man in the United States as Senate majority leader for the obscurity of a vice presidency. It was an office, he had once contended, that had been well described years before by a former vice president from Texas, John Nance Garner, that "being vice-president is not worth a warm bucket of spit."[93] But Johnson, because of his work with the U.S. Navy, was part of the military machine, and was also, in his new job, perfectly positioned to step into the presidency should something untoward happen to Kennedy.

Kennedy gave his reasons for the Johnson nomination to an aide during those hectic days. He explained,

"I'm 43 years old and I'm the healthiest candidate for president in the United States. *You've traveled with me enough to know that I'm not going to die in office.* So the vice presidency doesn't mean anything. If we win, it will be by a small margin and I won't be able to live with Lyndon Johnson as the leader of a small majority in the Senate. Did it occur to you that if Lyndon becomes the vice president, I'll have Mike Mansfield [a Senator from the western State of Montana] as the leader in the Senate, somebody I can trust and depend on '?[94]

'If Johnson and Rayburn[95] leave here mad at me, they'll ruin me in Congress next month. Then I'll be the laughing stock of the country. Nixon will say I haven't any power in my own party, and I'll lose the election before Labor Day. So I've got to make peace now with Johnson and Rayburn. '[96]

Johnson was elected as the vice presidential nominee on the first ballot the second day of the convention and the Kennedy-Johnson ticket went on in November that year to win the national elections.

Kennedy became President on January 20, 1961. He had come a long way in a short time, from congressman-elect in 1947 to President of the United States, all in 17 years.

The young president was unarguably videogenic. But though he performed outstandingly on television, he was inadequate for the world of *Realpolitik* and had a number of hard brushes with objective reality during his tenure in office. The last one was terminally disastrous.

His own reality was that of his heritage as a member of the finance-capital group. This fitted him poorly to deal with or even see what was really happening in the force world of the military-industrial complex.

Kennedy actually thought he was president, in fact as well as name. That was his tragedy.

The most serious threat to the military-industrial complex in the decades following World War II and the untimely death of Roosevelt was the multipronged attack mounted by Kennedy and his administration to *reduce the military,* just as Roosevelt had, and do away with its commanding role in American life. Mountains of trivia surrounding conspicuous men and events has been written about the Kennedys, particularly John F. Kennedy, who has been regarded as a person quite willing to use United States arms to maintain America's position abroad.

The facts do not bear this out.

As President, Kennedy actually presided over the beginning of what threatened to become a massive American military retreat worldwide and reduction at home.

General Marshall contended that diplomatic action without the backing of military strength would only lead to appeasement.[97] Kennedy's actions indicate that he did not recognize this dictum of Marshall's, but instead felt that speeches, economics, and a "dialogue between reasonable men" could provide the basis for worldwide diplomacy. And so he went from defeat to defeat, probably without realizing it, in the implacable world of *Realpolitik*. Kennedy, as president, permitted the sealing off, isolation of, and indeed the decapitation of East Berlin, a sound victory for the Russians, but presented to Americans as a sagacious diplomatic stroke.[98]

Neither did Kennedy grasp the full significance of Cuba. Fidel Castro, a ragged refugee terrorist who naively believed that Communism meant sharing the riches equally, won control of Cuba. Castro believed that communism could only be accomplished if the government was in complete control of the citizenry to ensure they could not acquire individual wealth, which is anathema to communism. The conquest was seen as a threat to the United States in that a Communist power was on an island stronghold a few miles distant from the United States mainland. This potential threat served the interests of the United States military-industrial complex in Washington in the continuing struggle to maintain a suitably high budget. It was a budget envisioned not to just survive, but to expand.

Kennedy never saw this. He thought the Pentagon actually wanted to free the island from Castro and so was led down the garden path of history to the fiasco of the Bay of Pigs.

The Bay of Pigs was a deliberately weakened invasion expedition organized by the Central Intelligence Agency that knowingly used well-meaning, but amateur, soldiers (Cuban exiles) instead of experienced combat troops. As if that were not enough, the effort was further muddled by changing the landing point at the last minute from Trinidad, Cuba, to the Bay of Pigs, and then to top it off, the situation was so strategized that adequate air cover was not provided, ensuring the failure of the mission.

The Central Intelligence Agency trained the Cuban force to be successful, which was supposed to work in conjunction with professional United States military forces. However, the invasion was attempted without United States forces, and failed, guaranteeing Cuba's continued survival as a Communist government under Castro. And thus it was that Cuba became a continual offshore threat to America. The feint by the military-industrial complex had succeeded. The military budget was increased. So long as Cuba remains a threat close to United States shores, the military is guaranteed a healthy budget.

After the Bay of Pigs, Kennedy reportedly stated he was determined "to splinter the Central Intelligence Agency in a thousand pieces and scatter it to the winds."[99]

Central Intelligence Agency Director Allen Dulles resigned a few months later, as did Richard Bissell, head of clandestine services. The shake-up affected others in the top echelons of the Agency and on down through the organization. [100]This mattered little because the military-industrial complex had accomplished its goal of ensuring that Cuba remained a threat to the homeland, requiring constant military readiness. The outcome was concomitant with Marshall's plan for an America designed as an alert, effective machine of war.

In yet another example of how Kennedy was deluded, in 1962, Khrushchev, the Russian premier, dueled with Kennedy in the matter of the Soviet move to ship missiles to Cuba, missiles capable of delivering atomic warheads to the mainland of America when launched from the island. The threat of a missile launch from Cuba would nicely justify a battle-ready American military. Kennedy challenged the Soviets on their claimed "right" to have missiles in Cuba. The Cuban crisis resolved when the Russians turned their Cuba-bound missile ships around in mid-ocean and took the lethal cargos back to the Soviet Union. Clearly, the Soviet Union was astute enough to not engage in a war, which could have escalated into a nuclear exchange.

And they smirked on the way home. They had plenty of other missiles aimed at the United States from Siberia and other points across the Asian continent. Actually, the Russians had lost nothing. United States losses surfaced the next year when, as part of diplomatic losses, the United States closed down and permanently lost her missile bases in Turkey and Italy. Kennedy was responsible. Had the missiles arrived and been installed, the military-industrial complex would have benefited enormously for a very long time.

The Cuban missile crises and its resolution was characterized by the finance-capital group as a personal victory for Kennedy. But the real victory was in the hands of the military-industrial complex because Kennedy was forestalled in his avowed intention to reduce the size of the military because Cuba has remained a threat, though a lesser one than missiles would have provided.

From the military point of view, the history of Kennedy's administration was a tapestry of wrong decisions, lost opportunities, misguided objectives, and badly managed crises. Worse, shortly before he went to Dallas in 1963, Kennedy issued a presidential order to make a cut in the American military presence in South Vietnam, with the immediate recall of 1,000 American soldiers back to the United States by the end of 1963.

President Kennedy's intended subsequent withdrawal of the balance of United States. soldiers in South Vietnam, about 12,000 of them, together with all the associated equipment a war requires, would have paralleled his 1962 decision in Laos where, by a negotiated peace and in tandem with Ambassador Averell Harriman, he had ended official United States involvement in that country by setting up a coalition so-called neutralist regime. That coalition would also have seriously affected the military because it was aimed at the complete withdrawal of American forces from South Vietnam. Getting the United States military out of that country was Kennedy's objective.

The military-industrial complex was watching and took note.

Kennedy had not worked out the mechanics of a United States-Vietnamese disengagement, but it was his stated intention that after he was reelected in 1964, he would take the risk of unpopularity by negotiating a peace, which would have been disastrous to the United States military.

But not if the United States military could prevent it. A covert operation took care of the first part of the problem in South Vietnam with the elimination of Diem. And then there was November 22, 1963 in Dallas, Texas.[101]

11:37 a.m.	Air Force One, the official presidential jet, touched down in clear and mild weather at Love Field in Dallas, Texas. The plane carried President John F. Kennedy along with his wife, personal staff, and various politicians concerned with his campaign tour through the State of Texas. Dallas was only one of a number of stops scheduled for the day. The big presidential limousine was waiting for them. It had been brought out from Washington, DC, for the campaign tour. Its bullet-resistant bubble top had not been installed and its bullet proof side windows were rolled down.
11:50 a.m.	President and Mrs. Kennedy seated themselves in the back seat of the limousine with Texas Governor and Mrs. Connelly in the folding seats in front of them. The motorcade left Love Field.

11:52 a.m.	The motorcade reached Mockingbird Lane.
12:01 p.m.	The motorcade turned down Lemmon Avenue to Turtle Creek Boulevard, then took Cedar Springs to Harwood Street.
12:20 p.m.	They turned West for a 10-block drive down Main Street, which was crowded with spectators.
12:22 p.m.	Main and Ervay Street.
12:24 p.m.	Main and Field Street.
12:29 p.m.	Main and Houston Street, where they turned right into Dealy Plaza.
12:30 p.m.	And then they turned a sharp left at Elm, where the open limousine slowed to 15 miles an hour. There was *no technical justification* for slowing down.
12:30:20 p.m.	With Navy Seal accuracy when shooting at a moving target from 90 yards away, Lee Harvey Oswald, who served in the Army Air Force in World War II, shot Kennedy twice in the space of 5 seconds. The first bullet hit the President in the neck. The second and fatal shot took blasted the right rear portion of his head away, which exposed his brain. At 1:00 p.m. Central Standard Time, he died in Parkland Hospital in Dallas, 29 minutes after first being hit.

Less than 1 hour and 40 minutes later, at 2:38 p.m. Central Standard Time, aboard Air Force One at Love Field, Lyndon Baines Johnson was sworn in as 36th president of the United States of America.

The presidential order to reduce United States military strength in South Vietnam by 1,000 men before the end of 1963 was still in force when President Kennedy went on his Texas campaign tour, which ended so suddenly. During the mourning period, just days after his assassination, the order was quietly rescinded by the new president: Lyndon Baines Johnson.

Lee Harvey Oswald, who shot Kennedy, was apprehended and jailed. Jack Ruby, with service in the U.S. Army Air Force in his background, in a hallway crowded with officers of the law, shot dead the now inconvenient assassin, Oswald.

The whole thing had all the earmarks of a military *operation*.

Ten years later, in 1973, the ever-increasing United States defense budget had reached $75 billion for the year, and in the decade after Kennedy's death, more than 3 million Americans saw duty in the armed forces due to the escalation of the Vietnam War.

Other examples of military-style operations at home and abroad include deaths of civilian leaders who have the temerity to suggest decapitation of the American military. The appalling statistics of wars throughout history[102] show a willingness on the part of military minds and others to sacrifice human life for political objectives. The military have never limited this expenditure of human life to just military lives, but have always included civilians—whatever element of the population they perceive to be standing in the way of victory.

Civilians observing or experiencing this military attitude toward human life often strenuously object, but in the end, the civilians remain . . . civilians . . . and the military continues to do the necessary rather than do nothing.

A case in point: Martin Luther King, Junior. King's most controversial speech was given as a sermon at the Riverside Church in New York on April 4, 1967. He was warned not to give it by members of his staff and family. King explicitly and with determination argued against the Vietnam War at a time when many Americans still supported it. He asserted that money was being lost in South Vietnam's killing fields that should have been spent on the war on poverty. In 1968, he decried, "A nation that continues year after year to spend more money on military defense than on programs of social uplift is approaching spiritual death."[103]

He was *anti-military.*

President Johnson cut off all communication with him. King was criticized by civil rights leaders, and some people told him to take his nose out of military affairs and stick to civil rights. King continued to oppose the war and fight for reduction of the military in nearly every speech he gave.

One year later to the day that his sermon was given at the Riverside Church, on April 4, 1968, King was assassinated in Memphis, Tennessee, by a certain James Earl Ray. Not unexpectedly, given the extent to which former members of the military are involved in sudden events that turn history, Ray had served in the U.S. Army in Germany.

Johnson had signed the Civil Rights Act 4 years earlier. Although the Civil Rights Act implemented the social justice aims of Martin Luther King, it did so without placing the military-industrial complex at risk.

It matters not who they are or where they are, if they have an audience of citizens, and if they proclaim that the United States military budget should be cut back or that military forces be removed from foreign soil or pulled off oceans or out of the air, they are at risk.

Section 8

MILITARY IN THE WHITE HOUSE TRUMAN TO CARTER

"History is the essence of innumerable biographies."
Thomas Carlyle,1795-1881

Men and women who join any branch of the armed forces spend their first few weeks in basic training. In the process of physical, weapons, and battlefield training, they become indoctrinated about the mission of the *Pax Americana*, the Form of war, and the corresponding world Form, but they are not called by those names. It is called basic training. Marshall knew the value of education and he influenced its curriculum. For the rest of their lives, graduates of military training programs tend to react to circumstances based on what they learned in highly controlled circumstances, what one might call brain-washing, about the role of the United

States as the dominant power among nations. They become and remain the troops of the self-sustaining phenomenon created by Marshall: a *Pax Americana*.

Only two of the last 12 presidents of the United States did not serve in the military: Clinton and Obama. Ten were indoctrinated in the mission of the military-industrial complex during training for their roles in the military. How did 10 men with military service wind up in the White House out of the 12 presidencies since World War II? Was it a coincidence of history? The proof of how they unconsciously served to keep peace at home and wage war elsewhere, the manifestation of Marshall's *Pax Americana*, is in their biographies.

This section and Section 9 have a minimum of citations to the literature because the facts are readily available in a multitude of publications. The one exception: reports of the budgets for the Department of Defense for each president.

Harry S. Truman (President from 1945 to 1953)

Truman served in the Missouri Army National Guard as an artillery officer in World War II.[104]The war revealed Truman's leadership qualities, for under his command in an active theater of war, primarily in France, his battery did not lose a single man.[105] Truman's war record launched his postwar political career that culminated in election as Roosevelt's vice president.

Truman assumed the presidency on April 12, 1945, when Roosevelt suddenly died. Germany and Italy had been invaded and occupied by the Allies, but the war with Japan was expected to take another year to accomplish, with enormous American casualties. Russia had become a problem because the ideology and spread of Communism was perceived as a threat to the United States by both Truman and Marshall.

Marshall became Truman's personal advisor on foreign policy matters.

Four months after Truman took office, on August 29, 1945, the United States bombed Japan with the first atomic bomb. Two weeks later, a second atomic bomb was dropped on Japan.[106]

Truman's bombing of the Japanese was not necessary to assure their surrender. Other methods without invasion were possible. But by *twice* bombing the Japanese with nuclear weapons, unheard of in world history, he showed the Soviets two things:

1. An absolute willingness to ruthlessly use the bomb.
2. That the United States had atomic bombs . . . not just *one* bomb, but many bombs.

When the war was over, Truman tripled the defense budget, approved the permanent partial mobilization of the armed forces, established a policy of globalizing the military and militarizing the homeland, founded the United Nations, and created the Department of Defense, the Central Intelligence Agency, and the National Security Council whose job it was to break encryptions on data and create encryptions for data.

Marshall was at Truman's side.[107] Marshall's vision to turn the United States into a *Pax Americana* was well under way with precise strikes, militarily and politically.

On August 29, 1949, 4 years after the first atomic bomb was dropped, Russian entered the nuclear community by detonating their first atomic bomb.

On August 7, 1953, Truman released the information that the United States had detonated a hydrogen bomb, and in so doing, announced to the world that it does not pay to engage in an arms race with the United States. The United States will always be ahead.

The haberdasher from Kansas city is unequaled in the American presidency because his decisions to use the best weapons the military had available was always fast and decisive. He bombed Japan less than 3 months after becoming president, he declared war on North Korea 2 days after Chinese troops were detected in the country and he threatened to obliterate them with atomic bombs if they persisted.

The fact that he disregarded the Congress is a testimony to his opinion of their use in a crisis.

When Truman took office, the defense budget was approximately $190 billion. When he left office, it was approximately $395 billion.[108][109]

Dwight D. Eisenhower (President from 1953 to 1961)

Eisenhower was a five-star general in the U.S. Army in World War II. He also served as Truman's chief of staff.[110] He followed Marshall's plan to send the military to foreign countries to squelch any perceived threat to the United States. He sent 15,000 troops to Lebanon to stop a pro-Western government from falling into the hands of an anti-Western group.[111] The move was reminiscent of the way Julius Caesar would send Roman legions to foreign countries to destroy threats to Rome before they could interfere with the homeland, all the while keeping the citizens of Rome entertained with spectacular exhibitions of butchery and murder while war was waged elsewhere.

A night with American television programming is a perfect parallel. Murder and mayhem are the entertainment of the night. Wars are elsewhere.

It is a strategy that is pursued to this day.

Recognizing the power of a nuclear arsenal, Eisenhower supported funding a proliferation of inexpensive nuclear weapons. This move allowed him to prudently reduce the size of any obsolescent military forces while reinforcing more advanced weaponry and fighting units.[112]

At the same time, Eisenhower recognized weaknesses in the military readiness of the homeland, the soil of the United States, to repel invasion and occupation. He proposed the Dwight D. Eisenhower National System of Interstate and *Defense* Highways that soon crisscrossed the nation.[113] The system of highways was designed not to support commerce, but to ensure that military armaments and men could be easily and quickly moved around the United States. He also created the Defense Advanced Research Projects Agency, the National Aeronautics and Space Administrations, and supported development of the peaceful use of nuclear power. A "peaceful" use of nuclear power would ensure a ready supply of weapons-grade uranium for atomic, hydrogen, or neutron bombs.

Toward the end of his tenure as president, and after experiencing the power of the military when combined with the power of the industrialists, he cautioned about massive military spending. It was a case of a genuine patriot recognizing for the first time what he had been part of his entire life without knowing it.

The Department of Defense budget during his presidency stayed at approximately $390 billion.[114]

John F. Kennedy (President from1961 to 1963)

Kennedy joined the U.S. Navy early in his adulthood during World War II. His induction was promoted by the director of the Office of Naval Intelligence, a former naval attaché to his father, Joseph Kennedy. He attended the Naval Reserve Officer Training Corps and then attended the Motor Torpedo Boat Squadron Training Center in Melville, Rhode Island. He was subsequently assigned to serve first in Panama and later in the Pacific war effort, where he became a lieutenant commanding a patrol torpedo boat (PT-109).[115]

In August 1943, Kennedy's boat, PT-109, along with two other boats, was conducting nighttime patrols in the Solomon Islands. Kennedy's boat was rammed by the Japanese destroyer *Amagiri*. Kennedy dragged an injured crewman through the water to safety with the man's life jacket strap clenched in his teeth. Kennedy was awarded the Navy and Marine Corps Medal. His other decorations were the Purple Heart, American Defense Service Medal, American Campaign Medal, the Asiatic-Pacific Campaign Medal with three bronze service stars, and the World War II Victory Medal.[116]

Military events during his presidency included the Bay of Pigs Invasion, the Cuban Missile Crisis, and an increased United States involvement in the Vietnam War. Then Secretary of Defense Robert McNamara asserted that Kennedy was strongly considering pulling out of South Vietnam after his expected 1964 reelection before he was assassinated. McNamara also revealed a tape recording of Johnson, in which he stated that Kennedy was planning to withdraw.[117]

It was a position that Johnson strongly disagreed with.

Kennedy signed a National Security Action Memorandum that ordered the withdrawal of 1,000 military personnel.[118] Once Kennedy was dead, Johnson deployed regular United States military forces to fight in the Vietnam War, which was the reverse of what Kennedy intended: to withdraw 1,000 troops.

The Department of Defense budget moved up to approximately $460 billion.[119] Never had military leaders been more comfortable, and it was a time of excellent business expansion for the defense contractors.

Lyndon B. Johnson (President from 1963 to 1969)

Johnson was in the U.S. Naval Reserve. During his World War II military career, Johnson became a commissioned officer starting in 1941. After asking for a combat assignment in 1942, he was instead sent to inspect shipyard facilities in Texas and on the West Coast. President Roosevelt subsequently assigned him to survey the southwest Pacific. A cloud obscures what happened during a subsequent survey mission. According to Johnson, the B-26 Marauder he was in was attacked by Japanese fighters. However, other flight crew members testified, and official flight records confirmed, that the plane returned to base due to mechanical trouble prior to any firefight with the Japanese. Nevertheless, General Douglas MacArthur awarded Johnson the Silver Star, the military's third-highest medal for valor.[120]

After the war, Johnson became a professional politician who served in several key posts in the government, including Senate majority leader.[121] He eventually gave up his powerful post as majority leader to become Kennedy's vice president. The vice presidency was a weak position, with virtually no power and no visibility. As to why Johnson made such move, it positioned him to take control should something happen to Kennedy.

Which did.

When he returned to Washington after the Kennedy assassination in late 1963 as president, he immediately focused on the military effort in South Vietnam. At that time, there were 16,000 American military "advisors" in South Vietnam. Congress obliged him by passing the Gulf of Tonkin Resolution. It provided Johnson with the exclusive right to use military force *without consulting the Senate*, and it set a precedent that would be capitalized on by a future president to start a war unilaterally. United States casualties by that time totaled 1,278. By March 1965, United States combat troops began arriving, and 3 years later, by 1968, 550,000 American soldiers were in South Vietnam.

Starting in 1967, 1,000 United States soldiers were being killed per month.[122] Johnson contended during his effort to build up the military in South Vietnam that the southwest Pacific desperately needed a larger share of war supplies. In his view, the Pacific fleet critically needed 6,800 additional men. He got them. In the same year, the Sixth Fleet was sent on a "training" mission where they could support Israel during the Six-Day War. There had already been United States ELINT and SIGINT (signals intelligence) asserts in the area. In all likelihood, the military -industrial complex saw the Six-Day War coming. It is doubtful, however, that Israel shared any advance notice with the United States.

The Soviets learned of this and proclaimed it as an offensive move. A message from Soviet Premier Alexei Kosygin laconically reported, according to the Secretary of Defense Robert McNamara, that he said in effect, "Mr. President, if you want war, you'll get war."[123]

But war with Russia was a no-win situation for the military-industrial complex, and the challenge was left unanswered.

Johnson left office on January 20, 1969, with a strong military-industrial complex in his wake. The Department of Defense budget had increased during his presidency to approximately $550 billion.[124]

Richard Nixon (President from 1969 to 1974)

Nixon served in the U.S. Navy in World War II. After taking office, Nixon initially escalated America's involvement in the Vietnam War by sending more troops and equipment to assist the Air Force, the Navy, and the Army.[125] At Nixon's invitation, Henry Kissinger became his closest advisor as his national security advisor and later Secretary of State. Nixon was a street fighter with a vocabulary to match and little notion of world Form. Kissinger was a brilliant scholar whose dissertation was about statesmanship, something Nixon knew nothing about.

Kissinger had served in the U.S. Army.[126]

The key to Kissinger is and always has been his doctoral dissertation because it was based on Spengler's *Decline of the West*, which was a theory about how the culture period we now live in is coming to an end at an escalating pace. A somewhat flamboyant writer, Spengler was, in fact, one of world's finest historians who detailed the rise and downfall of every major culture period known to man, and found similarities among them and to the present world culture. Kissinger's decisions as a diplomat were always based on Spengler's philosophical model of world power, which in turn was based on how culture periods are formed, mature, decay, and ultimately disappear. Just as the title of Spengler's work suggests, the culture period that dominates the world today is in decline. Managing statesmanship during the ending of the current period in the history of mankind was what motivated Kissinger in all his decision making.

Had Nixon ever read Kissinger's dissertation, he might have had second thoughts about appointing him his closest advisor.

Kissinger could not run for President because he was a foreign national born in Germany. He was a recipient of the Nobel Peace Prize and served both Nixon and his successor, Gerald Ford. Nixon became his pawn. For instance, following careful tutoring in foreign affairs by Kissinger, and then *bypassing his cabinet*, Nixon began interactions with China. Nixon sent Kissinger to China for secret meetings with Chinese officials. Finally, in 1971, it was announced that Nixon would visit China the following February.[127]

Kissinger briefed Nixon for over 40 hours in preparation for the trip. Then, in 1972, Nixon and his wife traveled to China. Nixon and Kissinger met with Mao Zedong, chairman of the People's Republic of China, and Zhou Enlai, first premier of the People's Republic, and they discussed many issues. Mao Zedong commented later that he was impressed by Nixon, but was suspicious of Kissinger. Nixon did and still does get the credit for neutralizing China, but Kissinger was behind it.

Kissinger began a campaign of what was to be termed "shuttle diplomacy" that required frequent travel to foreign countries. He kept war off American soil. And peace at home. And in so doing, in Kissinger, America had its first foreign-born president, in fact if not in name. Nixon was unsophisticated and worthless on the world stage. His attention was on the mundane, and his profanity and coarseness were legion.

Nixon concluded, with Kissinger's tutoring, that the Vietnam War could not be won and decided to end it. About 300 American soldiers were becoming casualties each week in South Vietnam when Nixon took office, and he was acutely aware that public opinion (so very carefully supported by the finance-capital group) was turning not just against the war, but against him personally. A withdrawal meant not just scaling back military involvement in South Vietnam; it meant reducing the military to prewar size. Nixon was the third president to make such an announcement: Roosevelt (dead), Kennedy (dead), then . . . Nixon.

It was the beginning of Nixon's undoing.

A military operation was in the offing.

In 1971, excerpts from remarks damaging to Nixon were published by *The New York Times* and *The Washington Post*. The papers indicated Nixon was behind a burglary of Democratic headquarters. Kissinger warned Nixon that the papers would be harmful to his presidency. Nixon tried to prevent publication, but the Supreme Court ruled for the newspapers. Indeed, Nixon's White House colleagues had engaged in an array of clandestine and often illegal activities related to the anticipated reelection of Nixon. Five men were caught burglarizing Democratic Party headquarters.[128]

Sniffing presidential involvement, reporters Carl Bernstein and Bob Woodward of *The Washington Post* published a series of articles that implicated Nixon. They relied on an informant dubbed "Deep Throat" for inside information. Impeachment hearings against the president culminated in a vote for obstruction of justice. With a long legal battle and impeachment looming, Nixon resigned his office. He had served 6 years.

Thirty years later, the informant who triggered the downfall of Nixon was revealed to be Mark Felt, associate director at the Federal Bureau of Investigation. He had no military experience, but perhaps acted out of an abundance of disgust with Nixon's crudity and utter disregard for ethics of any sort. Felt was later convicted of a felony for a civil rights violation unrelated to the so-called Watergate scandal, more or less a *quid pro quo* for Watergate, but Edwin Meese later advised President Ronald Reagan to pardon him. Edwin Meese served in the U.S. Army as a second lieutenant and in the Army Reserve as a colonel until 1984. They were all intertwined with the military-industrial complex in one way or another, except Felt.

The Department of Defense budget decreased during Nixon's presidency to approximately $395 billion.[129] It was a $55 billion reduction.

With Nixon ruined, the military-industrial complex turned to Ford, a more dependable source of sustainable power.

Gerald Ford (President from 1974 to 1977)

Ford's military career began in 1942 as a Naval Reservist. He loved the military milieu. At the U.S. Navy Preflight School in Chapel Hill, North Carolina, he taught basic military skills, earning a promotion to lieutenant. In 1943, Ford was assigned to the new aircraft carrier USS *Monterey* as an assistant navigator and anti-aircraft battery officer. In 1944, due to an onboard fire, the carrier underwent repairs, at which time Ford was detached from the ship. He coached athletics at the Navy Pre-Flight School at Saint Mary's College of California and the Naval Reserve Training Command, Naval Air Station, Glenview, Illinois, eventually being promoted to lieutenant commander.[130]

He became vice president during Nixon's second, truncated term of office, took over the presidency when Nixon left, and was elected President in 1973.

North Vietnamese forces in great numbers invaded South Vietnam in December 1974, soon after Ford took office. In response, Ford sent a $522 million aid package to South Vietnam and withdrew all United States military forces, not necessarily in the most orderly manner; the military-industrial complex had a lesson or two yet to learn. On April 21, 1975, Ford declared that, as far as America was concerned, the Vietnam War was over.

What followed was a Ford presidency characterized by frequent skirmishes with domestic policy and disturbances among, and with, foreign powers.[131] Kissinger, whom Ford kept on as Secretary of State, continued an intense schedule of trips to foreign capitals even though Ford considered Kissinger's continuing shuttle diplomacy "stalling." During Ford's term as president, Congress began to play an increased role in foreign affairs, as the finance-capital group had learned that packing the Congress with cronies was critical to their freedom to make money any way they chose. Congress also began a concomitant curb on the powers of the president, but was and still is not particularly successful based on future events. In 1976, a year after the Vietnam War ended, Ford defeated Ronald Reagan, former governor of California, for the Republican nomination, and then lost the presidential election to Jimmy Carter.

During the Ford administration, the military budget increased. The Department of Defense budget rose to approximately $410 billion.[132]

Nevertheless, the military-industrial complex continued to push for more, better, and bigger defense spending.

Jimmy Carter (President from 1977 to 1981)

Carter desired a career in the U.S. Navy from early childhood. He applied and was admitted into the U.S. Naval Academy in 1943. In 1947, Carter emerged with distinction after completing the accelerated wartime program. As an ensign, Carter was assigned to USS *Wyoming*, and later, the USS *Mississippi* for 2 years of surface ship duty, serving as radar officer and training and education officer.[133]

Carter then trained for submarine duty and was assigned to the USS *Pomfret* based at Pearl Harbor, Hawaii. In 1951, Carter served as executive officer, engineering officer, and later qualified as commander on the electric-diesel USS *K-1* submarine. Carter demonstrated a keen interest in developing nuclear-powered submarines. Promoted to lieutenant and detached from *K-1* in 1952, Carter was assigned to the U.S. Atomic Energy Commission, Division of Reactor Development in New York State, where he helped design and develop nuclear propulsion plants for naval vessels. In response to a nuclear reactor accident in Canada in 1952, Carter was placed in charge of the United States team assisting in its disassembly. This experience influenced his later presidential decision to not fund completion of the neutron bomb.

Carter resigned from the Navy and was honorably discharged in October 1953 to attend to family concerns. It is believed in naval circles that, had Carter remained in the Navy, he would most likely have reached the rank of admiral.[134]

Charming, soft-spoken, and calm, Carter was a sea change from the humorless, crude Johnson and the bluster and craft of Nixon.

Carter experienced a relatively quiet one-term presidency. On the domestic front, he created the Department of Education and the Department of Energy. He worked on solutions to high unemployment, inflation, and slow economic growth, conditions that always follow the expenditures of any war. As always, when Congress needed money to fight a war, they had raided the Social Security and Post Office funds, both a source of cash. The raids have continued to the date of this discussion in the wake of the wars in Iraq and Afghanistan. The endless raid on the Post Office has driven it to near bankruptcy.

Carter, without fanfare, pursued diplomatic solutions to problems outside the United States, and among other things, returned the Panama Canal to the country of Panama. The United States had appropriated the land for the canal many years before and ruthlessly oversaw the management of the canal.

Late in his presidency, four incidents eroded his popularity with the voting electorate. First, he had to deal with the Iran hostage crisis and oversaw a spectacularly failed mission to rescue the diplomats involved. Second, he had to deal with an energy crisis in 1979. Third, the Three Mile Island nuclear accident occurred, and the American people, as they always do when something goes wrong, blamed the presidency. Fourth, the Russians invaded Afghanistan, and Carter unwisely decided that American athletes would boycott the 1980 summer Olympics in retaliation. As a result, although he won the democratic nomination for a second term, he lost the election to the charismatic Ronald Reagan.

Carter cancelled military pay raises during a time of high inflation and government deficits, but the overall military budget remained at approximately $410 billion.[135]

Section 9
MILITARY IN THE WHITE HOUSE
REAGAN TO OBAMA

*". . . cutting the heart out of America's defenses is
like canceling all your fire insurance because you
did not have a fire last year."*
Casper W. Weinberger, secretary of defense
International Herald Tribune, November 29, 1989

What follows the observable end of a conflict is the
knowledge that, at the end, at winning, there is only losing.
Armies face winning with the sure knowledge that ahead
is the emptiness of "not doing anything," and having no
external focus. The entire structure of society falls idle in
winning: no need to make more weapons or support armies,
which puts untold numbers of people at risk of becoming
jobless. The driving engine, war, falls silent. By winning,
losing follows.

Far better to create yet another conflict.

In the moment when not doing anything faced the United States after World War II, Marshall created a *Pax Americana*: peace at home, war always, and always elsewhere. And so war has been pursued by the United States with vigor ever since.

Ronald Reagan (President from 1981 to 1989)

The military career of Ronald Reagan began when he completed 14 home-study U.S. Army extension courses in 1935. Six weeks later, he enlisted in the U.S. Army Reserve with the rank of private. Within 2 years, he was appointed second lieutenant in the U.S. Officers Reserve Corps of the Cavalry.[136]

Although he was nearsighted, Lieutenant Reagan was ordered to active duty in 1942, but was restricted to limited service. This classification prevented Reagan from serving overseas. He was assigned to the San Francisco Port of Embarkation at Fort Mason, California, to act as a liaison officer in the Port and Transportation Office.

In May 1942, Reagan applied for a transfer to the U.S. Army Air Forces, was approved, and was assigned to the Air Force Public Relations and First Motion Picture Unit in California. During World War II, over 400 training films were produced for the U.S. Army Air Forces under Reagan's direction. When he became president of the United States in 1981, Reagan also became commander-in-chief of all American armed forces, as do all presidents, and he relished the role.[137]

He was an actor, a horseman, a charismatic communicator, and military to the core.

Reagan used an escalation of the Cold War with Russia to order a massive buildup of all United States armed forces. The days of Carter's careful presidency were gone. Reagan revived the B-1 Lancer program that had been canceled by Carter and ordered the deployment of the Pershing missile in West Germany. He provided overt and covert aid to support anti-communist groups in Africa, Asia, and Latin America. He dispatched the Central Intelligence Agency to Afghanistan and Pakistan to help resist the Russian occupation of the former country, and to help prevent occupation of the latter.

In 1983, Reagan introduced a defense project entitled the Strategic Defense Initiative that ordered deployment of ground- and space-based systems to protect the homeland from attack by nuclear ballistic missiles from foreign countries worldwide. It was an extension of the program initiated by Eisenhower to weaponize the homeland so it could not successfully be invaded or occupied.

Reagan's foreign policies were called aggressive, imperialistic, and "warmongering." The military-industrial complex was in business again, unemployment was stopped in its tracks, and the vitality of the economy was restored.

During the Reagan presidency, the finance-capital group controlling the media found the likeable and photogenic Reagan hard to portray negatively. For one thing, he never took a bad picture in his life. When the media wish to shape public opinion against an individual, they choose the worst possible picture they can find to distribute, the more unflattering the better. There just were never any unflattering pictures of Ronald Reagan.

With the approval of Congress, in 1983, Reagan sent forces to Lebanon to reduce the threat of civil war which, if the wrong side won, could destabilize the region. Reagan sent a battleship to lob shells into Syria after a heinous attack on U.S. Army barracks in Beirut that killed 241 American soldiers and wounded 60. He ordered an invasion of Granada in the same year to bring down a Communist-leaning government. It was the first major military operation conducted by United States forces since the Vietnam War.

He was a hero to the military-industrial complex.

In 1986, he launched a very personal attack on Revolutionary Chairman Moammar Gaddafi of Libya, a strutting, bombastic leader of Libya for over 40 years. A Gaddafi-sponsored bomb had been set off in a Berlin cafe that wounded 63 American soldiers and killed one. The bombs that rained down on Libya were so aimed that they hit the courtyard outside of Gaddafi's residence, but did not touch the residence itself. His family was inside. Gaddafi often slept in a tent outside of the house, but that night he was not there. The bomb that hit the courtyard did not miss. It was a demonstration of the ability of the United States to precisely bomb a target with the correct payload and keep it exactly where they wanted it to go. The advanced technology of the military-industrial complex had been demonstrated as never before.

The attack was condemned by the United Nations. The response of the United States was indifference.

After the attack, Reagan declared, "When our citizens are attacked or abused anywhere in the world on the direct orders of hostile regimes, we will respond so long as I'm in this office . . . we have done what we had to do," Reagan threatened, and "If necessary, we will do it again."[138]

This was music to the ears of those in the Pentagon.

The Department of Defense budget shot up to $600 billion during his term in office, but slid back to approximately $550 billion before he left office.[139]

George H. W. Bush (President from 1989 to 1993)

George Bush decided to join the Navy as an aviator soon after the Japanese attack on Pearl Harbor. After graduation in 1942, he enlisted in the U.S. Navy on his 18th birthday. He was assigned to preflight training at the University of North Carolina at Chapel Hill. Graduating on June 9, 1943, he became the youngest commissioned naval aviator in the U.S. Naval Reserve.[140]

In 1943, Bush was assigned to Torpedo Squadron (VT-51) as photographic officer. Based on USS *San Jacinto* in May 1944, his Air Group 51 squadron routinely participated in Pacific operations against the Japanese.

In August 1944, Bush was promoted to lieutenant junior grade. He participated in bombing missions on Japanese communications and supply installations on ChiChi-Jima island. On what would become his final run, the Bush-piloted Avenger aircraft's engine caught fire from intense anti-aircraft fire. Bush completed the bombing mission, was hit, but still scored several damaging hits on the enemy with his engine ablaze. Bush and one other crewman managed to bail out, but the other man's parachute failed to open and he fell to his death. After a 4-hour wait in his inflatable raft,

Bush was rescued by the submarine USS *Finback*. Bush was decorated with the Distinguished Flying Cross for his effort.

After suffering over 50% pilot casualties, Bush's squadron was rotated out and returned to the United States. In just over 1 year, Bush had flown 58 combat missions and earned the Distinguished Flying Cross, three Air Medals, and the Presidential Unit Citation awarded to the *San Jacinto*.[141] His combat experience made him a natural fit for training new torpedo pilots. Later, he was assigned as a naval aviator in VT-153, a new torpedo squadron. After Japan surrendered in 1945, Bush was honorably discharged. A distinguished political career followed, during which he was elected president and assumed the office in January 1989.

In May 1989, 4 months after Bush took office, Panama held a democratic election, but the winner was quickly ousted by a rival. The issue for the United States was uninterrupted international use of the Panama Canal, one of the most important shipping passages in the world and critical to the movements of the U.S. Navy. Bush immediately sent 2,000 troops to Panama, where they conducted military "exercises." Bush closed the embassy and returned the ambassador to the United States, after which he sent even more troops to Panama to prepare for war. After a United States serviceman was shot by Panamanian forces in December of the same year, an incensed Bush sent 24,000 troops into the country to remove the insurgent president from power. It was a large-scale American military operation, and it succeeded.

That same year, in 1989, Bush met with Russia's General Secretary Gorbachev. No agreements were signed, but of interest, Gorbachev noted, "I assured the President of the United States that the Soviet Union would never start a hot war against the United States of America."[142] In July 1991, 2 years later, the Strategic Arms Reduction Treaty was signed by Bush and Gorbachev. The conditions in the treaty would reduce the strategic nuclear weapons of the United States and Russia by about 35% over 7 years.

This seeming reduction in force on the part of the United States was already unimportant, as the United States military weapons systems had long since far outstripped any such antiquated weapons as intercontinental ballistic missiles.

One year later, in August 1990, Iraq invaded its rich southern neighbor, Kuwait, and proceeded to sack the nation of all visible signs of wealth. The rulers of Kuwait begged for assistance from the United States. King Fahd of Saudi Arabia immediately requested United States military aid because he feared an invasion of his country as well. He invited the United States to organize an attack on the Iraqi squatters in Kuwait from his country, Saudi Arabia.

Operation Desert Shield was launched prior to an invasion. American Air Force fighters launched strafing missions and inflicted a superb pummeling with very sophisticated laser, radar, and GPS guided bombs and weapons. United States ground forces started their assault on February 24, 1991, and successfully ended it on February 28, 4 days later.

In a riveting press briefing on February 29,1991, General Norman Schwarzkopf asserted the United States had destroyed or rendered ineffective 29 Iraqi divisions on the way to freeing Kuwait. Iraq had 4,700 tanks and 3,700 were destroyed in 4 days. He acknowledged Iraq had 200,000 troops between the United States forces and Kuwait. He estimated there were 50,000 prisoners. When asked by a reporter what happened to the rest of the 200,000 troops, Schwarzkopf, in effect, shrugged, and then commented, "As far as Saddam Hussein being a great military strategist, he is neither a strategist nor is he schooled in the operational art nor is he a tactician nor is he a general nor is he a soldier."[143] Obviously,150,00 Iraq soldiers had died in 4 days.

The Iraqis were driven out of Kuwait.[144] Later, it was estimated that 3,664 civilians had also been killed[145] in spite of specific strategies that were used by the United States to *spare* civilian casualties. Extremely expensive guided weapons and on the ground intelligence were implemented to confine destruction to as small an area as possible. Drone handlers worked to target single terrorists by waiting to launch an attack until he was in a clear street or outside a village or city to avoid collateral damage.

The response of the United States in that brief engagement was unlike anything the nation had done before in terms of a massive, swift, ruthless, military operation.

In 1991, President George H. W. Bush asserted,
"A new era—freer from the threat of terror, stronger in the pursuit of justice, and more secure in the quest for peace [can emerge]. An era in which the nations of the world, East and West, North and South, can prosper and live in harmony . . . a world where the rule of law supplants the rule of the jungle. A world in which nations recognize the shared responsibility for freedom

and justice. A world where the strong respect the rights of the weak."[146]

An American president never sounded sillier.

Less than a year later, his naiveté was on display.

The next war in the region was Desert Storm in 1993. Bush received erroneous intelligence that Iraq had weapons of mass destruction, and he ordered an invasion. The United States sent Air Force fighter jets to control the air space over Iraq and to keep the eyes of the Iraq military occupied elsewhere while weapons and a massive buildup of United States forces began near Kuwait. The military-industrial complex welcomed an opportunity to test new weapons systems that had been developed since Kuwait was freed and to send soldiers into active duty to gain experience. The largely peacetime volunteer soldiers backed by hardened fighters from the war to free Kuwait swiftly defeated any resistance.

Shortly after his remark in January 1991, 4,000 bombing runs on Iraq targets were made by coalition aircraft with Bush's approval. The pounding continued until a ground invasion began the next month. New weapons were tried out, some to the delight of American Air Force pilots.

Bush cautiously stopped the offensive after 100 hours, saying he did not want to eliminate the Iraqi government because it would have "incurred incalculable human and political costs . . . we would have been forced to occupy Baghdad and, in effect, rule Iraq."[147] This astounding statement was made in homage to his earlier statement about "world peace." It left the dictator Saddam Hussein untouched to continue to threaten the United States. And so the United States withdrew with the job half done. Bush promptly lost the next election.

The Department of Defense budget decreased slightly during the Bush presidency to approximately $450 billion.[148]

Bill Clinton (President from 1993 to 2001)

Clinton was never a member of the armed services. The Clinton presidency resulted in the longest period of peacetime economic expansion in American history; however, skirmishes in foreign countries kept the military-industrial complex healthy and productive. In 1993, during his first year in office, the Battle of Mogadishu occurred in Somalia. Two United States helicopters were shot down by rocket-propelled grenade attacks, resulting in a battle that killed 18 American soldiers and wounded 73 others. After American bodies were dragged through the streets, United States forces were withdrawn. Two years later, in 1995, members of the North Atlantic Treaty Organization, a military alliance between European nations, Canada, England, and the United States, sent aircraft to pound Bosnian Serb targets to stop attacks on United Nations safe zones.[149]

Clinton, a brilliant politician and tactician within his own realm, was not altogether comfortable with the military, which resulted in convulsive and short-lived strikes overseas.

In 1998, Clinton ordered several military missions to capture or kill Osama bin Laden, a wily, well-financed terrorist who posed a threat to the United States both at home and abroad. They failed. Clinton next ordered cruise missile strikes on targets in Afghanistan and Sudan aimed at other terrorist targets. One year later, Clinton authorized the use of United States armed forces to participate in a North Atlantic Treaty Organization bombing campaign against Yugoslavia. Also in 1998, the military launched a 4-day bombing campaign against Iraq, during which American and British aircraft established no-fly zones. There were 166 such attacks on hostile Iraq air defenses in 1999, and 78 attacks in 2000. Clinton, by nature a pacifist, managed to survive his presidency without going to outright war anywhere.

But he was suspicious of the military and the military budget was falling. A scandal erupted about Clinton's unwise relationship with a young woman, which was trumpeted by the finance-capital group until Clinton was impeached. In this case, the military-industrial complex sat back and let the finance-capital group do the dirty business. It was a spectacular use of strategy to eliminate a target.

The Department of Defense budget decreased slightly during his presidency to approximately $410 billion.[150]

Once again, it was time to start a good war.

George W. Bush (President from 2001 to 2009)

The military service record of George W. Bush is blemished. Bush applied to become part of the officer corps of the Texas Air National Guard when he became eligible for the draft, which was scooping up young men at a furious pace, giving them some basic training, and sending them off to Vietnam. Acceptance would minimize his chances of being sent to South Vietnam. Despite his low score on the entrance exam, Bush was accepted.

In 1968, Bush signed a 6-year military service obligation that required him to attend at least 44 inactive duty training drills each year beginning July 1. After 2 years of active-duty service while training, he was sent to Houston, Texas, to fly an F-102 fighter-interceptor with the 147th Reconnaissance Wing from Ellington Field Joint Reserve Base between 1968 and 1973. Critics believe that, throughout this time, Bush was favorably treated because of his father's political standing, especially in relation to his designation as pilot and despite his low pilot aptitude test scores and his irregular attendance. Bush's own records indicate that he fell short of his attendance requirement, attending only 36 drills in 1972 and only 12 in the 1973.

In Spring 1972, while in Alabama, Bush was expected to continue his National Guard duties. His own records indicate that he performed no duty between April 16 and October 28, 1972, missed training in December 1972, and was absent again in February and March 1973. After failing to submit to an annual physical examination, Bush was removed from flight duty on August 1, 1972. No records exist of him having *ever* served with any unit in Alabama.

National Guard members earn two service points per weekend training-day and are required to accumulate a minimum of 50 service points a year. In May, June, and July, 1973, Bush spent 36 days on duty, accumulating 41 points, but was mysteriously awarded 15 gratuitous service points to vault him past the 50 service points requirement. Although his last service day was July 30, 1973, 6 months short of his November 1974 mandate, he was honorably discharged early to allow him to attend Harvard Business School. He also attended Yale and afterward worked in the oil business.

Based on these shady and shallow credentials, he was elected as governor of Texas in 1995, after having failed earlier to be elected to the House of Representatives.

His was a reckless presidency, but it provided the military-industrial complex with their largest budget increase in the history of the nation. He was putty in their hands. Eight months into his presidency on September 11, 2001, the World Trade Towers in New York City were destroyed by terrorists. Nine days later, Bush launched what he termed a War on Terror. Using Truman's declaration of war on North Korea without congressional approval and Johnson's Gulf of Tonkin Resolution that provided him with the exclusive right to use military force without consulting the Senate as a precedent, Bush demanded and got emergency powers from the Congress so he could defend America without the time required to go to Congress, and those emergency powers exist today, where they are apt to remain unchallenged, as will be discussed in the next section. United States and British forces invaded Afghanistan, which was perceived to be the homeland of the terrorists who leveled the World Trade Towers. The main goal of the war was to defeat terrorism on its home ground. It did not succeed. In spite of escalating the number of troops and equipment over the years to suppress the Taliban, they prevailed. Six years into the war, in an effort to end it, Bush sent 3,500 additional troops to Afghanistan, to no avail.

Internationally, Bush managed to weaken the widespread levels of international support for the United States that followed the September 11 attacks by asserting both a right and an intention to wage preemptive war at will. His rashness was hardly a secret. The United States became what could only be termed a warmongering nation, a charge last leveled at Reagan by the international community, but this time it was deserved.

In 2002, Bush re-focused his attention from Afghanistan to Iraq and described the country as "a grave and growing danger" to the United States because of the supposed possession of weapons of mass destruction, which turned out not to be the case. In 2003, Bush launched a new invasion of Iraq based on the faulty intelligence that Iraq had weapons of mass destruction. Later, when he ordered the abandonment of efforts to find Osama bin Laden who was responsible for the destruction of the World Trade Towers, Bush sniffed, "I really just don't spend that much time on him, to be honest."[151] He added that "focusing on one person really indicates to me people don't understand the scope of the mission."[152] The statement was classic Bush arrogance.

What power was behind the faulty intelligence that Iraq had weapons of mass destruction, and how could the Central Intelligence Agency have made such an incredible mistake? Or was it a mistake? In any case, the military-industrial complex capitalized on the mistake.

After massive expenditures by the military and total occupation of Iraq, no weapons of mass destruction were found. In 2007, Bush followed the advice of his joint chiefs of staff and ordered a surge of 21,500 more troops to Iraq, and later vetoed a bill that set a deadline for an end to the conflict. Clearly, he was a water boy to the military-industrial complex.

In 2008, General David Piraeus openly recommended *withdrawal* from Afghanistan. Petraeus failed to understand that his reasoned decision spoken openly would lead the military-industrial complex and their aide-de-camp Bush to ensure his downfall by whatever means were available, which he inadvertently provided by having an affair. The media were alerted, and he was relieved of his command after a furious campaign of character assassination.

Never threaten to cut the military budget.

During his presidency, the aggressive, belligerent Bush authorized the National Security Agency to monitor communications between suspected terrorists outside the United States and suspects within the United States without obtaining a warrant, as required by the Foreign Intelligence Surveillance Act. He authorized the Central Intelligence Agency to use water boarding, a form of torture, on suspected terrorists. He signed a law that allowed the United States government to prosecute captured enemies by military commission rather than a standard trial, a law that denied them access to *habeas corpus*, and allowed the president to determine what constituted torture. The law has never been rescinded.

Bush *vetoed* a bill that would have provided enhanced Congressional oversight over the intelligence community and approved the use of water boarding and other forms of interrogation specifically banned under the United States Army Field Manual on Human Intelligence Collector Operations. He dallied with North Korea until May 2009, when an annoyed North Korea restarted a closed-down nuclear program and threatened to attack South Korea. He enforced economic sanctions on Syria and Lebanon, withdrew United States support for several international agreements, and denounced the leader of Palestine. He announced support for Taiwan against Chinese intrusion, and authorized United States military intervention in Haiti and Liberia. Support for Taiwan provided potential access to undersea oil in regions whose ownership remains a bone of contention between Taiwan and the Peoples Republic of China.

Incredibly, in 2008, Bush asserted Russia's invasion of Georgia was bullying and intimidation and not the way to conduct foreign policy in the 21st century. He applied his definition of bullying and intimidation to others, not to himself, but he was the biggest bully on the planet.

The Department of Defense budget skyrocketed to an all-time high of approximately $900 billion[153], just shy of $1 trillion, during his presidency.

Barak Obama (2009 to present)

Obama was never a member of the armed services.

During his election campaign, the finance-capital group, having survived the 2007 recession wealthier than ever and believing the presidency was within their grasp, supported Mitt Romney for president. Romney was the perfect figurehead for the finance-capital group, a ruthless corporate raider without a trace of a conscience who reaped profits for the pure pleasure of it, regardless of the cost to others. Corporate raiders buy companies and then strip them of as many assets as they can, including retirement funds. He revealed his mindset toward the citizenry when he made a remark during his campaign for president that he thought would never be seen by the public. It was a word-perfect statement of the finance-capital group's philosophy toward anyone not part of the 100 men who control two-thirds of the money in the United States.

He smirked,

"There are 47 percent of the people who will vote for the president no matter what. All right, there are 47 percent who are with him, who are dependent upon government, who believe that they are victims, who believe the government has a responsibility to care for them, who believe that they are entitled to health care, to food, to housing, to you-name-it. That's an entitlement. And the government should give it to them. And they will vote for this president no matter what."[154]

This offensive statement tainted his campaign for the presidency.

Obama won handily. It was a demonstration of the precise process that will eventually bring down the oligarchy and with it the United States in its present form.

The United States defense budget began to shrink within a year after Obama took office and will continue to shrink while he is in office. Influencing the downward plummet was first, the end of the war in Iraq, and second, the withdrawal of troops and equipment from Afghanistan. Obama declared in his campaign for president that he would end the two wars, and he did. He has been parsimonious about engaging the armed forces, but when presented with an opportunity to kill Osama bin Laden, he swiftly and decisively approved a military operation that could have easily failed for a number of reasons. The military budget continues to drop because the 2011 Budget Control Act, referred to as the "sequester" and backed by the finance-capital group's pawns in Congress, ordered the Pentagon to enact hard budget caps and cut defense spending by approximately $1 trillion in the next 10 years.[155] The Department of Defense budget in 2009 was approximately $720 billion when Obama took office, but sank to approximately $640 billion by 2012.

Based on history, Obama is in danger if he opposes an outright war, which would revive the military budget.

Roosevelt, dead, Kennedy, dead, Nixon, banished, Clinton, shamed. Obama?

Has the danger to him already started?

To whose interest is it that the Secret Service, established in 1865 and tasked with guarding the President in 1905, and after 109 years of exemplary service and untarnished reputation, inexplicably became so lax that armed men and imposters suddenly got through the screen of security around Obama to within striking distance? One fired on the White House with a rifle, which the Secret Service did not detect at the time. Another, a phony translator for the deaf, stood next to him making senseless signs while the president delivered a speech.

Obama's fate is yet to unfold.

Section 10
THE WEAPONIZATION OF AMERICA

"War in the future will concentrate on a single objective: rapid, complete, and unscrupulous annihilation of the enemy."
Rowan, Spies and the Next War, 1936

Modern warfare, which is waged in terms of who has the greater technical capability, is characterized by the importance of developing weapons, not by the winning of battles. Thus, there is a technique to be developed for each element involved in winning—the spy satellite, the drone, the cyber-spying—every conflict calls for development of a range of techniques to win. The focus of business, industry, and government in developed nations is not peace; it is winning the inevitable wars needed to guard the status quo.

The path to peace is too littered with conflict to exist in the realm of possibility. This is true for all nations on earth with resources they wish to protect; hence, the need for ever more advanced weaponry. This truism is validated by the following eras:

World War 1 (1914–1918) 4 years
World War II (1939–1945) 6 years
The Korean-Vietnamese War (1950-1975) 25 years
Desert Shield and Desert Storm (1990-1991) 1 year
The Iraq War (2003–2011) 8 years
The Afghanistan War (2001–2014) 13 years
The ISIS War (2014–ongoing) 1+ years

Ninety-nine years of conflict. Fifty-eight years of outright war.

War is the American ethos. The spirit of the age. The *Zeitgeist*.

War abroad and peace at home was the pattern Marshall envisioned to ensure American global domination. He took steps to put the process in place before the end of World War II, and he succeeded. A *Pax Americana* of his design is in place and functioning and it mimics what happened in Rome. The making of the *Pax Romana* began when Augustus accepted the responsibility for providing peace at home for Romans who had been continuously at war for decades,[156] just as America has been at war for decades. Augustus was the first to define the *Pax Romana* when he told Romans that they could only have peace at home if enemies were fought elsewhere, well before they posed a threat to the homeland. Thus it was that the Roman legions were sent out far from

Rome to knock down any threat to the Empire, which resulted in 200 years of peace and prosperity at home[157] just as American armed forces are sent out globally to quell perceived threats to the United States.

While maintaining a strong military presence abroad after World War II, Marshall was determined to equip the homeland to repel foreign invasion from the north, south, east, or west. Nations invade other nations for three reasons: to obtain resources or wealth, to acquire new territory, or to eliminate threats to the homeland. To achieve any of these objectives of war, invasion and occupation must take place. Marshall's objective was to make the continental United States a machine of war that no invasion of any size could destroy. This is why the threats of Islam are so laughable. Islamists are geographically isolated where they are, with no means to invade anything but their neighbors.

In a brilliant strategic move to counter the Islamists, almost all United States military actions in the Middle East have served *to foment unrest* in that region, *not arrest it*. This strategy has focused Islamists on their inter-faction disputes and directed their external actions not toward the continental United States, but toward the European Union. Although the United States wages war in the Middle East for the professed purpose of freeing the area from brutal dictators, it wages no campaigns to free other countries with brutal dictators. Militarily, it is a brilliant tactic.

Invading and occupying America with enough men and equipment to control the population would be a formidable challenge, in part because of geography. From the west, invading forces would face a vast desert often 500 miles wide that stretches from lower Idaho into central Mexico, a nearly impossible military barricade restricting the movement of men and machines because of the difficulty of the supply chain needed to support an army across hundreds of miles of barren land. From the north, it would be equally difficult because 90% of the population of Canada live within 50 miles of the border—for a reason. Beyond those 50 miles, the land is a vast expanse of permafrost that forms an impassible military barrier. From the east, the concentration of population for the first 500 miles inland from the coast would render the movement of large armies and supply chains difficult and slow. From the south, the Gulf of Mexico is bordered by swamps for most of its length from Corpus Christi to Florida.

The second line of defense, and to ensure failure of any attempt to invade the United States, military and industrial leaders set about preparing the United States homeland as a weapon of war just as if it was a cannon or a bomb. As a result, the prevailing mission of the military-industrial complex is to keep the United States military weaponry 15 years ahead of every other nation in the world, including battlefield readiness of soldiers, sophistication of weaponry, ferreting (spying) capability, and maintaining the homeland in a state of readiness to repel invasion. Following are some examples of how the homeland has become a machine of war.

The War Powers Resolution of 1973

Technically, under the U.S. Constitution, war powers are divided. Congress has the power to declare war, raise and support the armed forces, control the war funding (Article I, Section 8), while the president is commander in chief of the military and the National Guard (Article II, Section 2). The Constitution gives the president the power to repel attacks against the United States. The president is responsible for leading the armed forces. The president also has the right to sign or veto a declaration of war by the Congress.

During the Korean-Vietnamese War, the United States became involved with no Congressional approval having been issued. Congress took notice when it became known that President Nixon conducted secret bombings of Cambodia during the Vietnam portion of the war. He had not told Congress about his military plan.

They let it pass.

Starting a war by ignoring the Constitution has been done by enough presidents to set a precedent.

Yet another way to circumvent the Constitution has arisen. After 60 days of United States combat in Libya, President Obama notified Congress that no congressional authorization was needed because United States forces were under NATO command. Marshall would have approved. If the United States is attacked, or United States interest is to wage war, the president can activate the military against the enemy without authorization, including use of the atomic bombs against the aggressor, *so long as NATO is involved.*

The Interstate Military Highway System

President Eisenhower authorized the Dwight D. Eisenhower National System of Interstate and *Defense* Highways.[158]The word *Defense* has since been dropped and it is now known as the interstate system. Civilian use was not a consideration during its design and construction.

When construction began on the interstate highway system, to an outside observer, it must have seemed curious that this network of north-south and east-west widely divided highways were funded at all because the volume of civilian traffic, particularly across the vast territory from the Mississippi River to West Coast, was light. The overpasses were the first to be built because crossroads are where armies are stopped in their tracks in wartime, as was shown in both World War I and World War II. Crossroads are bottlenecks. So the overpasses were the first to be built because they formed the most critical part of the military highway system. It was a strange sight to drive down an old two-lane highway and look across a field of corn or wheat and see a massive overpass out in the middle of nowhere with nothing but dirt tracks leading up to it and away from it.

The interstate lanes each way are widely separated by a grassy medium, which is a military design. No conventional bomb can destroy the movement of vehicles because there is plenty of room to go around such obstacles. The network of military highways permits convoys of equipment and troops to be easily moved from coast to coast and from the Mexican to the Canadian border. Especially important was to surround the Rocky Mountains zone of the interior with military highways because they would be the last bastion of defense of the United States should the rest of the country fall.

Thus began the weaponization of America.

Military Bases

The country has 51 Army bases, 61 Air Force bases, and 53 naval bases, widely dispersed, by plan, around the continental United States. The Marines, because they are a strike force, maintain over 50 points of departure around the world. It would be a formidable task to cripple all American military installations at the same time. The United States also, as of this writing, has 450 Minuteman intercontinental ballistic missiles in silos primary located in Montana, North Dakota, and Wyoming.

In addition, the United States maintains battlefield-ready submarine-launched ballistic missiles. The battlefield that has emerged in the 21st century is in a configuration that is highly driven by electronics, which could be crippled with an electromagnetic burst; however, the need for invasion and occupation remains if any foreign power wishes to occupy the United States.

Wiping out any piece of this machine of war would be like stabbing a bear with a pocket knife. It would just make the bear mad. Kissinger argued, "Wars of the 19th century and the total wars of the present are the signs of an age which attempts to wrest out of chaos its version of truth, its vision of law, its intuition of permanence"[159] All this is happening as the people of the world try to find balance in an unbalanced world.

Peace is a dream. War is the reality.

The Federal Acquisition Regulations

If the United States Congress were to cut defense spending, it would curtail all the military services, reduce readiness, and cast aside many of the elements of the strengths that keep America safe. It would reduce all defense contractor budgets and cause widespread unemployment. Any threat to defense spending poses a threat to the nation, both militarily and economically.

Thus it is that the Department of Defense is home to the biggest military procurement budget on the planet.

Standing firmly between any threat to the nation— and the longevity of the military-industrial complex—is a self-sustaining phenomenon, referred to herein as the *Pax Americana*, that Marshall envisioned. Any attack on the military-industrial complex by either a domestic or a foreign power is met with resistance whether by open warfare or subterfuge. Keeping a balanced fighting force is partly the job of the contracting agents in the Pentagon.

The Armed Services Procurement Regulation (ASPR) was created after the end of World War II in 1948 as a direct result of abuses of the government contracting process by both politicians and industrialists. The ASPR contained the mechanics of maintaining a weaponized America. Before the ASPR, cost-plus as a percentage of cost contracting was the norm, down and dirty, with rampant profiteering, fraud, and theft, not to mention the usual *quid pro quo* that was prevalent behind the scenes when Congressmen were special advocates for industries in their districts or states. It was not that nobody cared during World War II; it was that oversight was not the primary mission, which was to win the war at all costs. It was not until World War II was won that corrupt procurement of military supplies could be addressed with new legislation and regulation.

The ASPR established that cost-plus percentage of cost contracts would end a contractor's business with the military—they became, and still are, illegal. They still exist in certain narrowly defined and exigent circumstances, but the decision to permit the use of them is made at the highest levels of government and they are ruthlessly monitored for abuses.

The ASPRs were followed by the Federal Acquisition Regulations (FARs). When a unified regulation was announced, the logical answer was to pull the civilian agencies such as the Environmental Protection Agency under the Department of Defense, logical if standardization of acquisitions across agencies was to be accomplished. However, the civilian agencies balked; they did not want to be subject to the FARs. Civilian agencies did not want to be burdened with detailed requirements and heavy oversight of their medicines, their energy studies, their environmental clean-ups, their low-dollar value (read: unglamorous) buys. But neither did the Department of Defense want to be burdened with addressing and monitoring civilians' vastly inferior procurement practices or to be associated with the routine off-the-shelf nature of most of it. In the end, the Department of Defense became responsible for procurement for all acquisitions remotely associated with the military establishment under the FARs. As soon as the FARs were published, the civilian agencies immediately began setting up their own individual regulations to exempt or distinguish themselves to avoid the FARs.

So much for standardization.

In addition to the procurement of supplies, weapons, and research, the Department of Defense is home of procurement of the exotic, the special, the classified, and the crucial to the national defense. Classified procurements are done as exceptions to the FARs, not quite out of sight completely, but monitored by key personnel under secure conditions and not the subject matter for the Defense Acquisition Regulation Council, which is the successor to the ASPR Committee.

In spite of the mountain of words that have been published about the FARs, there remains the question of how they are actually applied (when there are no wars to fight) to the defense industry to keep the military-industrial complex from so much damage through reduction of production that the nation would lose its military capabilities and subsequently succumb to a sudden attack by a foreign power.

To maintain equilibrium of the military, procurement officers in the Pentagon have a list of all the defense contractors in the United States, big and small. The primary spreadsheet contains every procurement every contractor has received, whether it was a cost overrun, an on-time delivery, or was accomplished according to the original contract. The data were recently turned into a database, the Federal Oversight and Implementation Act of 2014, that is a public record accessible through the Contractor Performance Assessment Report. The overall health of contracting organizations and their locations are carefully monitored.

Everything is tracked, including the place where the production facility is located because the location of a production facility can cost a contractor a job. If the nation were to be attacked by a foreign power, it needs to be able to continue manufacturing an item even if one plant is obliterated. For instance, if all airplane manufacturing was done in one city, one atomic bomb could end the capability to produce airplanes altogether. Thus, one defense contractor located close to another contractor, both of whom manufacture the same thing, is dangerous to the nation's security because one good bomb could take out both of them. However, with the manufacturing capability for military goods spread out from coast to coast, it is impossible to destroy the ability of the military to re-arm itself unless the nation itself is geographically leveled. Consequently, location of a facility is a key discriminator in the award of contracts.

The development of industrial clusters, which is the intense geographic concentration of firms such as in Silicon Valley, are dangerous to the nation's security. Nevertheless, authors unconcerned with defending the country, tout the value of such clusters.[160][161][162] Industrial clusters, also termed industrial parks, allow firms to pull from a common and accessible pool of resources. Although the clustering of firms is likely to facilitate the leveraging of commonly needed resources, if one bomb can obliterate an entire cluster or park, they are a danger to the survival of a nation at war.

As well, it is to the advantage of the military-industrial complex if all the primary defense contractors can be kept in a healthy and productive state of readiness. To address this need, if a contractor has not received a contract for a while, but its name is on the list of viable, approved, and *necessary* contractors, sooner or later, it will get a turn, no matter what sort of bid it submits. The lowest bidder does not always win.

The industrialists and the military cooperate to keep the United States in a state of war readiness at all times. Marshall intended it to be that way. At times, this measured award of military contracts is at odds with the wishes of politicians in the House and the Senate, who mount vigorous efforts to keep contracts in the district or state in which they are elected and reelected. Their shortsightedness is legion.

Oblivious to the needs of the nation to defend itself, the finance-capital group keeps its focus on money, now in a global playground. It is the military-industrial complex that is the glue that holds the United States together.

Homeland Security

The Homeland Security Act of 2002 contained language that promised it would make the nation "safe, secure, and resilient against terrorism and other hazards."[163] The Homeland Security Agency was charged with the responsibility to "reduce America's vulnerability to terrorism and minimize the damage" from any attacks that do occur. It was provided central authority over 187 federal agencies to ensure efforts were coordinated in case of an emergency.

Significantly, the Department of Defense is not a member, nor is the Federal Bureau of Investigation or the Central Intelligence Agency. The term "homeland security" pertains primarily to the civilian aspects of protecting the nation, while the term "homeland defense" pertains to the military. Some crossover occurs in certain circumstances. Of note is that the Homeland Security Act provides, among other things, the authority for the Homeland Security Agency to put every airport in the United States under central government control. Thus, every airport can be commandeered by the military and shut down in an instant.

So far, the powers of the Homeland Security Agency have only been visible after natural disasters and during coordination of search and rescue operations and other non-security activities. A curious upshot of the Act is that citizens, after Hurricane Katrina, interpreted the Act to mean it would provide them with alternative permanent housing if their homes were destroyed, and they became incensed when new homes were not provided. The Agency, to keep the peace, provided trailers for people to live in, but even those came under attack. A self-righteous and entitled public shifted the blame for their discomfort on the new and inexperienced federal agency that was still learning what it could and could not do. Interestingly, in terms of the attitude of the citizenry toward the military, it was not until soldiers showed up that the foment was quieted.

The Power Grid

The power grid in the United States is a military defense-offense weapon. It did not start that way. An electrical grid is a network of power generating stations that crisscross the nation. The network can move power from city to city, region to region, or from one side of the nation to the other. While the average person has been led to believe this is to satisfy consumer demand, it is a powerful military weapon, either to support a particular region or cut off a region, for instance, in the case of invaders.

Interest in electricity dates to the year 600 when it was noticed that certain activities produced static electricity such as rubbing amber or rubbing an animal's fur. The generation of static electricity was studied widely for centuries, but the birthplace of today's electric power began in 1600 in England with William Gilbert, who published *De magnete, Magneticisique Corporibus*(on the magnet), in which he explained his research and experiments with electricity and magnetism. Gilbert coined the word "electra," which in later became "electricity." The book raised the interest of many scientists, who explored the possibilities of electrical power generation.

One-hundred fifty years later, in 1750, Benjamin Franklin flew a kite to prove that lightning was electricity. Unfortunately, he is given far too much credit in today's history textbooks for "inventing" electricity when, in fact, many scientists from many different nations had been studying electricity for over 1,000 years.

By 1878, when electrical power first began to power homes, businesses, and military operations, it was the result of isolated power generation capabilities. Each town, once the power of water was discovered as a means of creating electricity, would build a community power station on a nearby stream or river. While many of them were owned by the community, many also were owned by individuals.

Controlling the availability of power in the United States after World War II became a military necessity because of the need to control the supply of power, ever more so today because of all the power-needy electronics within the weapons system.

The "power grid" movement began in 1878, when Edison Electric Light Company in the United States and American Electric and Illuminating, the latter of which was founded in Canada, were organized and began acquiring all the small-town power generating stations they could buy or steal. The public was a captive audience for power and profits were there to be made. One year later, in 1879,the first commercial power station was established in San Francisco and the first hydroelectric power station opened in Wisconsin. By 1886, Westinghouse Electric Company reported it had 40 to 50 water-powered electric plants on line or under construction in the United States and Canada.

Another example of how power grids came into being was in the state of Utah, which was replicated across the nation.

Mormons entered Utah what was a Federal territory, beginning in 1850. In a state devoid of any settlers except a few eccentrics and murderous trappers, each small town was established close to a source of water so settlers did not have far to go from the forts they built to protect themselves from Indians—who took exception to their presence. Twenty-eight years later, the first hydroelectric power generating system was built, and leaders in Salt Lake City saw an opportunity to generate electricity and lift their population out of darkness. In 1881, the Salt Lake City Light, Heat, and Power Company opened its doors. Salt Lake City was the fifth American city to generate power from a central station.

Once the hydroelectric technology was introduced in Utah, all the small towns in the state installed their own small electricity plants on the streams that were so near. Many are still in existence, mostly as historical curiosities, because Utah Power and Light put all the small-town power generating plants out of business. Deliberately.

General Electric set up the Electric Bond and Sharer as a holding company to buy or steal small power companies in Utah, Idaho, and Colorado so they could sell General Electric's power equipment. Eventually, the holding company owned more than 200 power companies in 30 states, which meant by the 1920s, they controlled 14% of the power in America.

Utah Power and Light eventually acquired 130 small power companies in Utah and Idaho. When the United States geared up to fight World War II, Utah Power and Light expanded to meet the electrical needs of the state's new military bases and defense-related companies. Nine separate military bases and facilities in Utah were in need of power, as well as the Geneva Steel Plant in Utah County that the federal government built to supply steel for defense contractors. Private companies engaged in producing weapons in Utah at the time were the Remington Small Arms Plant, the Eitel McCullough Radio Tube Plant, and the Standard Parachute Company. Hill Air Force Base was added in 1939. In 1958, Utah Power and Light began participating in the development of atomic energy. Along with 51 other utilities, it formed the High Temperature Reactor Development Associates to fund research and development.

As power grids came into being, at the same time the military increasingly needed power for electronics, and also control of the power grid as a defensive weapon.

Tying even more area into the existing grid, in 1987, Utah Power and Light and PacifiCorp announced they had agreed to merge in a $1.85 billion stock swap. Utah Power and Light became a subsidiary of PacifiCorp, which used Utah Power and Light to sell power to California and the Southwest, and the grid expanded exponentially. In 1998, it was announced that Scottish Power, based in Scotland, attempted to purchase PacifiCorp pending approval by the Securities and Exchange Commission, the Nuclear Regulatory Commission, the Federal Energy Regulatory Commission, and state regulatory bodies. The military-industrial complex was not about to let it happen. The sale was cancelled.

The same story of the formation of the grid was duplicated around the nation. As a result, within minutes, the military can turn off the power in the entire nation within minutes. They can shift power from one region to another, or focus all of it in one area. The need for quick access to huge power reserves by the military has led to studies of the possibility of subterranean storage of electricity in naturally occurring strata. Such storage would be beyond destruction by any enemy.

The power grid has become a military weapon.

Gun Control

An armed populace cannot be easily occupied. In Japan during World War II, every Japanese citizen was armed, if not with a gun, then with a sword or a pitchfork, and they would have fought for their homeland, which would have cost thousands of lives on both sides of the conflict. Two atomic bombs ended that eventuality.

To maintain the *Pax Americana*, the military-industrial complex cannot support a disarmed, demilitarized population if the nation is to defend itself should invasion occur. Japan was a perfect example of the problem with an armed civilian population. The mass casualties on both sides would have made invasion of Japan a slaughter of unimaginable proportions.

The military-industrial complex prefers that every man, woman, and child have a gun. Admiral Isoroku Yamamoto, architect of the attack on Pearl Harbor said: "You cannot invade the mainland United States. There would be a rifle behind each blade of grass."[164]

Any nation that lusts after America's wealth or territory could turn 10 American cities into glass with hydrogen bombs, but if they tried to occupy the land, they would still face a nation where every remaining citizen, young and old alike, had a gun and would use it. And would do so until every last citizen was dead. Anyone who does not believe that the spirit of the American people would cause them to resist an occupation to the last living soul able to lift a hand in defense is naïve.

The fight over gun control began with President Johnson. As a professional politician, Johnson was caught between his concern about an upcoming election and failing popularity if he signed the Gun Control Act on October 22, 1968. He signed it grudgingly. The Act was one of the largest and most encompassing federal gun control laws in American history. In part, with a nation reeling from the assassinations of John F. Kennedy, Robert F. Kennedy, and Martin Luther King, Jr. gave Johnson little choice. After the assassinations of such publicly loved individuals, the reaction of the people opened a vitriolic fight about gun control.

The most iconic picture of the fight against gun control was Charlton Heston, the actor, when he raised a rifle above his head and snarled that the gun would only be removed from his "cold, dead hands."[165] Heston enlisted in the Army Air Forces in 1944. He served on a B-25 bomber in the Alaskan Aleutian Islands with the 11th Air Force. After the war, he held the highest security clearance available at that time—the Q clearance. He was the perfect embodiment of the military-industrial complex.

The doctrine of self-defense, as it pertains to individuals, is as old as civilization, but the idea that only the state can possess the arms necessary for self-defense has its roots in the conditions following the European fratricidal religious wars that culminated in the Peace of Westphalia in 1648.[166] Traditionally, in the world before the advent of the nation and state, arms were hand-made and very expensive; therefore, only the wealthy and governments could afford to possess them on a large scale. The peasantry might be mobilized and given weapons to fight specific engagements, but when the battles were done, the arms were collected from the survivors and stored against future use. As a result, a tradition of private gun ownership never became widespread in Europe with two exceptions, one of which was in Britain. In the United Kingdom and her established colonies, known as the Anglosphere (America, Canada, Australia, and New Zealand), the tradition of private ownership of guns has always been extremely robust until the last 20 years of the 20th century.

Because life on the frontier in America was so perilous, private gun ownership was a feature of American life. As technology improved, guns became more numerous, more standardized, and cheaper, allowing more people to obtain them.[167] One of the acts of the first U.S. Congress in 1789 was to pass the Bill of Rights as part of the first 10 amendments to the Constitution. So important was the right to bear arms that it was the second numbered amendment. As a constitutionally protected right, it is unique among world constitutions and will remain an *almost* insurmountable barrier to gun control forces, both domestic and foreign. Indeed, it would be to the advantage of any nation wishing to defeat the United States to disarm her citizens. Given the fact that foreign nations can now donate funds to political candidates for office, it is not unimaginable that certain members of Congress could mount a withering attack on the people's right to bear arms.

Legally, the Constitution and its amendments control *federal* behaviour, not that of the state. Prior to the passage of the 14th Amendment, which appeared to make the Bill of Rights applicable to all states, states and communities were at liberty to enact gun control or not. Many states did, in fact, incorporate the individual rights provisions of the federal Bill of Rights directly into their state constitutions, but it was not a uniform practice. The principal method of control after the Constitution was written was and remains a requirement for gun owners to be licensed or permitted by local law enforcement officials.

It is unenforceable.

In 1934, the federal government enacted the first national gun control legislation by banning private ownership of fully automatic weapons in the aftermath of the St. Valentine's Day Massacre, a gangster-driven elimination of rivals. The government assigned federal gun control policy to the Bureau of Alcohol, Tobacco, and Firearms. But it was the assassinations of President John F. Kennedy, his brother Robert F. Kennedy, and Martin Luther King, Jr. that galvanized gun control advocates and began the modern political battle over individual gun ownership.

While the gun control lobbies diligently pursue restrictions, the American public is largely politically passive about the matter. The citizenry only arises in response to a tragedy. The assassination attempt on President Ronald Reagan produced the Brady Act, an effort to place national restrictions on hand guns.

It has not worked.

Massacres in California and New York resulted in the 1994 Assault Weapons Ban that applied to military-style weapons and high-capacity bullet clips. It had a 10-year sunset provision, after which the act expired.

Efforts to revive it have been unsuccessful, most recently after the Newtown School massacre in December 2012.

Voters may say they favour gun control in the abstract, but repeated exit polling demonstrates that fewer than 10% of voters base their votes for specific candidates on the candidates' positions on gun control.

In a relatively recent imaginative approach, gun control advocates have sought to make gun homicide a public health issue. Because gun ownership is a form of elective behaviour, this initiative has sought to force that behaviour into a pathological disease model. It is posited that gun owners are not engaging in a constitutionally protected activity; they are victims of a pathology.[168] Control advocates have funded "research," which has been greeted enthusiastically by the scientific community, to create studies that prove gun ownership is indeed a "disease," and the only "cure" is confiscation. Doctors and other health professionals have been encouraged to speak out against the scourge of guns as they were once encouraged to speak out against the scourge of malaria, polio, influenza, and sexually transmitted diseases.

The military-industrial complex cannot afford to have the citizenry disarmed. But alas, the gun control advocates within and outside of government are clear about what they want: banishment of handguns, or preferably all weapons, from the hands of the citizenry.

The finance-capital group does not care, but they will, one day. Once again, when the survival of the nation itself is at stake, their focus is on manipulating global stock markets in an up and down pattern, where vast amounts of money can be made in milliseconds. Meantime, public officials, opinion leaders, government agencies, scientific authorities, media outlets, and famous private citizens have been enlisted to propagandize the public against the freedom to own guns, an important constitutionally protected right and last line of defense if the nation is attacked.

But gun control advocates are beginning to experience decreasing success because the U.S. Supreme Court finally addressed the issue of the Second Amendment's protection of an *individual* right to bear arms. After a hiatus of almost 70 years, the Supreme Court accepted the case of *District of Columbia v. Heller*, 544 U.S. 570(2008)and ruled the District's ban on guns, its requirement for disassembly or implementation of a device that effectively made the weapon unusable when not in active use, was unconstitutional. The Court held that the right to own guns for self-defense was subject to reasonable limits consistent with state interests that were not contrary to the underlying purpose of the Amendment. Unfortunately, the decision applied only to the District of Columbia, and because the District is not a state, a second case was required to make the holding in Heller applicable to every state. *McDonald v. Chicago*, 561 U.S. 742 (2010)

was brought before the Court and the Court held that the Second Amendment applies to the states, making private gun ownership lawful, but subject to reasonable regulation.

Regardless of the efforts of gun control advocates, the military-industrial complex will, in the end, ensure that every citizen can own a gun. The security of the homeland depends on it. The prospect of an invasion and occupation against a disarmed population cannot be allowed to happen.

In summary, the influence of the military-industrial complex extends to these and many other aspects of the life of the American citizen. It is ever-poised to explore new avenues with which to equip the nation against all threats, including internal ones. From it have arisen 10 of the last 12 Presidents, not a coincidence. It influenced the way the interstate highway system was built and is maintained or extended, where military bases are located, how and to whom government contracts for weapons and defense systems are funded. It stands by to take over homeland security in an instant, ensures that the power grid is sustainable and moveable from one region to another, and quietly blocks gun control so every citizen can be ready to fight an enemy with something other than a pitchfork or a baseball bat. Its surveillance and spying capabilities are unmatched, as is its ability to collect data from ground-based operations and space-based satellites. It is formidable, implacable, determined, and ruthless. It is the sum of its parts, and it dominates the world.

Section 11
WAR WITHOUT SOLDIERS

"If I had seen a ghost, I should have looked in the
very same manner, and did just as he did."
Henry Fielding, Tom Thumb the Great, 1707-1754

In the history of mankind, it has always been dangerous to be a rich nation. Standing in the way of an enemy's intent on acquiring the United States is the military-industrial complex, the most effective fighting machine since the legions of the Roman Empire. It is a complex that will win against all enemies, utterly, at any cost, that possesses the most sophisticated intelligence-gathering technology in the world as well as weapons that can turn any city, large or small, into glass.

Only winning matters.

Boots on the ground is an anachronism, a form of war bypassed by the advance of a sophisticated and ever more deadly and secret weaponry. Following are a few of the operations that are carried out to avoid putting soldiers in harm's way. They were initiated to sustain the military-industrial complex, but the finance-capital group has adopted them with devastating effect when used against the population, they who have a rapacious appetite to make more money, and to them, the end justifies the means.

Data Mining

Data collection and data mining are two different things. Data collection is the gathering of data from every conceivable aspect of the known world, and data mining is combining and recombining that data into meaningful information that can be acted upon.

These weapons of war are not new.

Data mining operations by the industrialists such as American car manufacturers has been going on since Henry Ford faced his first competitor. At every car manufacturer's "research" facilities in America are huge garages where every make of car in the world is up on a rack and being taken apart piece by piece and analyzed. That is data collection. Car manufacturers' analyze all their competitors' products at a furious pace, and compare it to what they have or have not—that is data mining. They are seeking ways to bury their competitors by offering the same thing or something better. The American way is to buy a competitor's product and take it apart for any new ideas it might contain that can be used.

In the same manner, the military-industrial complex and the finance-capital group are both engaged in a deadly game of data collection and mining, but for different purposes.

The military use data to protect the nation. The financiers use the data to make money.

The methods for collecting and mining data continue to soar in sophistication. For instance, the Hubble telescope is orbiting earth pointed outward toward the farthest reaches of the universe to where new galaxies are being discovered every day and captured in crystal-clear pictures. If Hubble is pointed outward, logic informs that there is another Hubble also in orbit. The other Hubble is pointed in the opposite direction, earthward, and taking crystal-clear pictures.

It is data collecting.

And Hubble is soon to be supplemented by the James Webb Space Telescope, *100 times* more powerful than the Hubble.[169] The ability to see what is there is a military weapon of unimaginable power.

Just as the United States has ultra-sophisticated satellites, enemies of the United States also have satellites. Logic again informs that if a foreign power has a satellite that could pose a danger to the United States in a conflict, the military-industrial complex has a satellite whose mission it is to destroy it. Foreign-owned satellites are only safe as long as the United States wishes them to be.

Serious data collection by the military is best characterized by the Federal Bureau of Investigation when the organization began collecting a copy of every fingerprint taken in the United States since before World War II. Tracing a fingerprint in the database is 99.6% accurate. More than 120 million individual computerized fingerprint records comprise the bulk of the database, drawn from both criminal and civilian records, and there are 20 million pictures of individuals, many of them conveniently supplied by the social networks. As well, palm prints, face, and eye/iris pictures, DNA samples, and a range of other identifying markers find their way to the largest repository of such data in the world. This provides the military with one part of a vast database with which to stay informed about who is in the country, who supports the country, and who needs to be dealt with for one reason or another. The finance-capital group also maintains a vast repository of information about people. Some of it is based on common census data that allow them to predict, block by block in every American city and town, how much money people have to spend and what they will spend it on.

Law enforcement depositories are insensitive to whether someone has been arrested and then found not guilty. Once the fingerprints are taken for any reason, they are sent to the Federal Bureau of Investigation. Old paper fingerprint cards are manually maintained. Enlisted military service members' fingerprint cards received after 2000 have been computerized. But the military has not stopped there. *Anything* posted on the media is being collected at a furious pace.

The finance-capital group has also discovered the use of data collection and mining, and although they do not have the capacity to collect information as broadly as the military, they are using what they have to acquire money from every possible source available.

Twenty-eight years before revelations about data mining were initially exposed in 2006, when *The Washington Post* and *The New York Times* trumpeted Bush's security efforts to track terrorists through financial networks, a 1978 Supreme Court decision ruled individuals had no privacy rights to stop their personal information from becoming part of metadata bases.[170] The ruling forestalled any effort in 2006 and afterward to disband the practice. The magnitude of data collection and mining is a 21st-century ethical dilemma. The ethical dilemma is that these huge databases, while they serve both the military-industrial complex and the finance-capital group, also pose a monumental threat from enemy nations who can use such information to propagandize the people of the United States, or worse, to control the people should the United States fall. An enemy would not need to identify those they wished to eliminate with patches, as Germany did to their Jewish citizens in World War II. Every citizen on the Internet puts a badge on themselves.

The only way to circumvent the decision is to get the 1978 decision reversed by the Court.

Where data mining is concerned, it is obvious that there was some kind of National Security Agency information vacuuming program long before the 1978 Supreme Court acted; otherwise, there was no need for the decision to be rendered in the first place.

There are multiple millions of cameras in America recording and archiving footage of people going to the bank, shopping in stores, pumping gas, entering and moving around hospitals, walking down residential streets, monitoring traffic lights, and so on. In fact, stepping outside one's front door may mean stepping into the view of a camera, and the numbers of those cameras are increasing. Drones survey anything stationery cameras cannot catch. The cameras register every face that boards a plane or attends a sporting event or goes up the gangway to a cruise ship, and the photos become part of the primary database. Passport and driver's license pictures are archived, credit card information, bank records, cell phone calls, residential addresses, and all other forms of identification or communication are copied and archived.

Every citizen of the United States today has a profile somewhere in the databases of the military -industrial complex or the finance-capital group, and the use of that information is not under the control of the citizens.

Data mining happens after collection, when the many bits and pieces are coalesced into a whole picture of an individual, or a corporation, or a mom-and-pop business, or a worker in the fields. As well, within the next 5 years, the United States will be able to create a profile of any individual in every developed nation on earth, and many undeveloped ones. What they look like, what they buy, what they eat, how they dress, who their friends are, who they talk to, what they think, how they spend their time, where they work and what they do at work, and hundreds of other details brought together to present a complete picture of anyone the military-industrial complex or the finance-capital group wishes to know about.

In a frightening development, the marriage of data mining to the field of psychology enables the assessment of an individual's capabilities, weaknesses, and probable actions. Militarily, this provides leaders with the ability not just to spot potential threats, but also to forecast the intention of every person in the United States and anyone abroad that arouses their interest.

In Utah, an enormous complex is currently being built by the military-industrial complex to house the vast quantities of data collected from around the world. Even in the wake of the revelations of Edward Snowden, the collection of data on the minutiae of everyday life for every single United States citizen as well as foreign nationals continues in the name of protection from terrorism.

Moving "off the grid" is a pipe dream. Off the grid does not exist.

Spying

As was said by Sun Tzu in *The Art of War,* 4th century B.C., "The essence of war is deception."[171] Spying is the gathering of information. Sabotage is done after spies have acquired information about tactical or strategic assets, specialists have analyzed what damage could or should be done to an asset, and politicians have decided which assets should be damaged or destroyed. Being sent to assassinate someone is not espionage. It is the action decided upon after analysis of information gathered by spies. Politicians maintain plausible deniability in relation to an assassination because they are the public eye.

Spies are everywhere. The military-industrial complex has their own phalanx of them, and the finance-capital group has even more sitting in offices around the globe analyzing competitors' assets and deciding which ones require attention. Spies operate with the same ruthlessness as when a battlefield is active, whether it be Wall Street or Iraq. Spying is just another form of combat. Militarily, in 1936, Rowan stressed,

> "When everybody appears disturbed about the next war, it is reasonable to ask how many are aware of the one now going on. Governments . . . persistently engage in their old subterranean conflict, a prolonged skirmish of vast mobility and well-dissembled ferocity, at once ancient in origin, medieval in cunning, and ultra-modern in technique."[172]

Nothing has changed since 1936 when Rowan made his remark.

Spying is portrayed as a dark, but glamorous occupation. It is perceived to be an inviting blend of danger and glamour, heroism and sex, murder and deceit, and it always comes out well in the end. In truth, it is often a lifetime of waiting with no results, mountains of information with no clear answers, and incidents so disparate that they make no sense. Inevitably, the spy is exposed to the constant danger of discovery. Corporations spy on other corporations by sending their spies out to take jobs with a competitor. Nations spy on each other by sending their spies out for information and to assess weaknesses. It is laughable when the media wonder out loud how the Central Intelligence Agency could miss a mass meeting of Al Qaida and an opportunity to drone-bomb them into extinction. Detractors fail to think that the Agency knew about the meeting and had one or more spies in the group. One does not exterminate a spy successfully inserted into an enemy group.

Spying takes several forms: sabotage, propaganda, intelligence, and counter-espionage activities, all of which can be managed either with a person collecting information or with electronics, all of which are conducted by both the military-industrial complex and the finance-capital group.

Sabotage. Militarily, disrupting communications, the flow of information, and the movement of supplies needed to support the citizenry or the military is one aim of sabotage. Railroads, fuel supplies, main highways, satellite communications, electronic data storage, and power transmission are targets. Reducing food resources by damaging cropland and distributing propaganda about the safety of food are common targets of propaganda. Comparatively, so too does the finance-capital group disrupt communications, the flow of information, and moves money to achieve its objectives.

Damaging or destroying enemy manufacturing capability is an inviting target for sabotage. Iran's nuclear program was seriously damaged when 1,000 centrifuges were disabled in an intentional cyber warfare attack implemented with the Stuxnet computer worm. Stuxnet was designed to infiltrate and take over control of industrial systems and was specifically designed to target Siemens industrial control systems. In the case of Iran, which had acquired Siemans equipment covertly—which is of no historical importance—Stuxnet caused the centrifuges to spin wildly upward beyond their capabilities while, at the same time, showing controllers that the equipment was operating normally. By the time the centrifuges began to fail, 1,000 had been ruined.

In a different realm, the finance-capital group undermines or invades the computer systems of a competitor to gain advantage. Cyber-attacks are commonplace.

Militarily, damage to military depots, ports, stored supplies of raw materials, and any other resource needed for supporting a battlefield or a population of people are targets. Attacking financial systems is a top priority and is usually accompanied by propaganda aimed at disturbing people about the security of their finances. The finance-capital group actively engages in propaganda to assure people that their money is safe, when in fact, it is not.

Attacking municipal power plants also disturbs people because power is critical to their lives, and this damage is particularly effective when combined with propaganda that causes people to become uneasy about their safety. Oil reserves, water supplies, and transportation, when disrupted, weaken an enemy, as does any attack on gasoline, coal, or gas. Defending against sabotage of these resources is critically important for the military-industrial complex, while damage to an enemy's resources is a top military maneuver. The finance-capital group, in this instance, is forced to support the objectives of the military-industrial complex because their survival depends on these basic resources.

A campaign to influence people to believe they are underpaid and overworked is sabotage and includes the release of reports of shortages, unequal wages, and political malfeasance. The finance-capital group works hard to convince people that their investments are safe, and they are quick to defeat stories about political wrongdoing if the politician is one they have financed. Sabotage also includes biological warfare. In 1918, when World War I ended, it was revealed that the Germans had developed a fountain pen that could be loaded with cholera or another agent of death and carried unobtrusively into crowded public places, where the contents could be easily released upon surfaces such as door handles. The Germans were on the verge of carrying out such an attack on Russia, and only the end of the war stopped them. The problem with this type of sabotage is that weaponized agents are unconcerned with national borders. This type of sabotage is currently self-defeating because of the rapidity with which large numbers of people move from country to country. The deadly agent could devastate the perpetrator just as easily as the target.

Propaganda. Propaganda is a mental attack on a population, designed to artfully light the fire of public opinion. Propaganda is the life's work of politicians and the handy work of the finance-capital group. The bombardment of propaganda upon the citizenry in the United States today is intense, clever, continuous, and effective.

When propaganda comes from an external source, it is a menace that leads the military-industrial complex to spying on its own citizens and results in the regulation of communications and the movement of people, industries, and supplies.

The successful distribution of propaganda is enhanced by the degree to which people believe erroneous information, which is especially easy today because of the extent of social media, such as Facebook with its 1 billion registered users, Twitter with 500 million users, Formspring with 290 million users, Linkedin, with 200 million users, Google+ with 500 million users, and dozens of lesser known sites such as Bebo with 117 million users, or BlackPlanet with 20 million users. A spy has only to start a rumor in one of these social media sites to propagandize them all.

Militarily, rumors about food or water supply shortages, failure of financial institutions, rumors assailing the government or government leaders, and exaggerating an enemy's intentions or capabilities—such as the propaganda that justified the Iraq war—are all forms of propaganda. Sources for destabilizing the population are easily spread today through the media, and the general population, with their tablets and cell phones and computers, are blithely unaware of it.

Intelligence. When people see pictures of the main buildings housing the National Security Agency, and particularly the Central Intelligence Agency, they are misguided into believing that the size of the buildings indicates the number of spies in the field, those so gloriously personified by Hollywood and in novels. Instead, the buildings house an army of researchers. They research all day. They are not sent out on assignments in foreign countries to pilfer information, enlist double agents, or maintain observational platforms. They just research. The ratio of researchers to actual spies operating in foreign countries is thousands to one. The reality of the National Security Agency and the Central Intelligence Agency is not that they are Ninja-style spies with secret weapons; they are nerds and geeks with computers collecting data, assessing data, and looking for patterns.

Penetration of opponents by establishing spies in their midst is one focus of intelligence gathering, whether it be sponsored by the military-industrial complex or the finance-capital group. But intelligence gathering is also aimed at protecting personnel, installations, and operations. Just as the satellite eyes of the United States are turned toward every nation in the world for data collection, one of the missions of military intelligence is also to turn inward and search throughout the nation for internal threats to personnel, installations, and operations. So, too, does the finance-capital group gather intelligence on a global scale the better to anticipate market weaknesses or strengths worldwide, the better to ensure profits.

The activities of the spies, both military and civilian, in foreign countries are focused in several specific areas. They are the watchers. In the military, they watch mobilization of military forces, where they are stationed, and keep track of the placement of the weapons of war, such as planes and ships. In the financial capitals of the world, the financiers watch the development of corporations and market shares of nations and governments. Militarily, the watchers keep current on the development of weapons, armies, resources, and information-gathering capabilities. They monitor civilian morale, interests, and the degree of intent to harm the United States. They observe the stability and intentions of governments, their military, and groups of people. The financiers monitor any operation or circumstance in the world that might be a threat or might be a source of additional income.

Spies, both military and civilian, spread propaganda. They infiltrate as necessary, and often remain in place in foreign governments, or in corporations that are competitors, for many years. When possible or perceived as a need, members of the military-industrial complex become "handlers" and enlist foreign nationals into the service of the United States. In the case of the financiers, they enlist a competitor's employees into aiding them. Such handlers are extremely manipulative, and have raised the activity to an art form. It is their job. Eventually, many become toxic to their assignments, and are returned to the United States or returned to their home corporations to serve in other capacities until they retire.

Counterespionage. Spies, both military and those arising from the finance-capital group, also engage in counterespionage, but it is a highly specialized field and calls for extraordinary skills of observation, manipulation of information, and insight. Insight is the ability to synthesize information, often fragmentary, and extrapolate facts. Insight is a skill once taught in American schools, but abandoned when the focus turned to more testable skills such as mathematics.

The primary focus of counterespionage is the interception and destruction of any effort to sabotage any of the elements of national or corporate security, to mitigate propaganda, and to stop any individuals or materials that could pose a threat internal or external to the United States, or to the corporation or organization under attack. The extent to which the various federal agencies in Washington have information and share it with others is the extent to which counterespionage is successful, and the same is true of organizations. Espionage can involve all of the elements of sabotage, intelligence gathering, and spying.

The military-industrial complex perceives of itself as the protector of the nation. The finance-capital group perceives of itself to be above the struggle for survival of the nation. Locked in a battle for control, yet caught in a symbiotic relationship, the war between the two rages.

Only the military-industrial complex keeps the nation as it was intended by the Constitution:

We the People of the United States, in Order to form a more perfect Union, establish Justice, insure domestic Tranquility, provide for the common defense, promote the general Welfare, and secure the Blessings of Liberty to ourselves and our Posterity, do ordain and establish this Constitution for the United States of America.[173]

Section 12
OTHER MEN WILL COME

"Only the dead have seen the end of war."
Plato, 424/423 B.C.–348/347 B.C.

Use of the word "conspiracy" postulates something, some established entity against whom one conspires. But in the world of practical reality in which we actually live, in the politically formless era of our lifetimes, there is no established political order against which to conspire. American "democracy" is inherently formless, an experiment only 200 years old, and the more so as it continues its course down the generational sequences. In a sense, all the active parties in the democratic struggle are conspirators, each striving to achieve power to effect their own configuration on the world against all the others, but in the classic and generally used sense of the word, they are not conspirators.

As far as American politics are concerned, the use of that word by anyone is a matter of purely autobiographical importance.

The revolver in the hip pocket of America has always been a tradition of ever-evolving machines of war, and that tradition constitutes a decisive force in American politics. This is truer than ever today in the era of electronic-based warfare with the devastating power possessed by a military ready to use it.

Organizations are living phenomena,[174][175] just as the United States is a living phenomenon and has the same characteristics as a living entity. Organizations ingest and digest raw materials they need to survive. They extrude waste. They think. The movement of information in organizations is how they assess their well-being—meetings, status reports, memos, e-mail traffic, procedures, annual reports, mission statements—and in the case of the military-industrial complex and the finance-capital group, data collection and data mining.

On a global scale.

Organizations have both conscious and unconscious processes. Over time, activity that may, at the beginning, have been conscious, planned, and executed with deliberation by human hand takes on a life of its own, outside of conscious awareness.[176] Marshall's plan to create an America dominating the world was, in the beginning, a strategy, but 68 years later, the plan he created is manifesting itself through unconscious norms and basic assumptions, completely out of view.

The necessary actions to sustain it arise naturally, unassisted by conspirators.

The *Pax Americana* evolves, regenerates, and self-organizes to adapt to changing circumstances. Like other complex adaptive systems, it evolves constantly, but changes are self-organized changes, a process by which a structure and pattern emerges without that change being directed from outside.[177] Living systems learn and use new information to alter present and future behavior. A living system, such as the *Pax Americana*, is constantly balancing and rebalancing to maintain homeostasis.

The simplest way of understanding the *Pax Americana* is that it manifests itself whenever the whole is smarter than the sum of the parts. A collective phenomenon can arise and be different than the components that comprise it. People spontaneously organize themselves to create organizations that no individual may intend, comprehend, or even perceive.[178]

The military-industrial complex is the protector of the *Pax Americana*. It is they who maintain the health and welfare of the United States by waging war. Kissinger commented, "equilibrium is achieved not by the fact, but by the consciousness of balance. And this conciseness is never brought about until it is tested, and the most total test can come about only by war."[179]

War is the spirit of the age, as envisioned by Marshall and commented upon by Kissinger. Since the year 1700, over 100 million people have been killed in war, 90% of them in the 20th century.[180] More are yet to die.

Marshall's *Pax Americana* is today a living system comprised of a set of components that work together for the overall objective of the whole. It is geographically dispersed and is unconsciously supported by millions of Americans. It is complex and adaptive. It is open because it collects information from the environment, it uses these data to create plans, it learns, and it takes action based on that learning. It has a memory, an identity, and has created processes to accomplish its mission.[181] It will evolve, always with its mission in focus, which is to sustain America as a machine of war and keep armed conflicts off American soil.

It is the Form of the culture of the United States.

Ten of the last 12 Presidents were in the military. Coincidence? No. The self-sustaining phenomenon created by Marshall has become a collective thought process engaged in by an entire nation of people. The collective consciousness of America produces a response without any meetings behind closed doors of conspirators bent on controlling circumstances. Marshall's plan for the future of the United States succeeded and it has become part the culture. It has a life of its own. It has became a living thing that no one can see, and it silently controls the country.

Marshall's understanding of what created and what destroyed great civilizations led him to the conclusion that peaceful, militarily equal coexistence with any nation of equivalent power, in our times, was a pipedream, and that inevitably, one nation would prevail over all others. Marshall intended that nation to be the United States.

As for the continuing threat of Russia, Marx was a professional revolutionist. He saw the world from below, by design adopting the perspective of his concept of a "proletariat." Proletariat is a counter concept of Marx's "Capitalist." His was an outlook, not an overlook. The objective of that which he created was and always has been to subvert and to overthrow the West and her ways. Despite disclaimers and dissimulation, Russia's policy today is a continuation of Great Russian expansion that periodically and persistently threatens the West. As for China, she is not a threat to the United States because, although she has billions of people with which to launch a massive invasion, China is economically tied to the United States. Unbalancing that economy would destroy the economies of every other nation on the planet, and China would be the first to fall.

There is, indeed, a relationship between where the United States is today, headed for an *Imperium*, an empire, and where Rome was at approximately the same point in the unfolding of history. Some comparisons prove this point, particularly in the 41 years between 27 B.C. and 14 A.D. in Roman history.

Just as the United States began as a republic, the government of Rome was a republic encompassing the entire area surrounding the Mediterranean and including Greece, North Africa, Spain, and France. Prominent in the move toward an *Imperium* was Julius Caesar, a highly successful military leader who followed in the footsteps of several other military leaders who acquired countries and city-states for Rome through military action and subsequently controlled the government because the people trusted their military leaders. This parallels the phenomenon that 10 of the last 12 presidents of the United States have been veterans of military service. Americans choose presidents who have military experience because they have a deep-seated trust in them above candidates from any other background. In the 2016 presidential election, the political party that proposes a candidate with military experience and who has name recognition will be elected above any candidate who does not have military experience in his or her background. History proves it.

It is the *Pax Americana* in action.

The first body of men controlling the affairs of Rome were those in the Roman Senate. There were 300 men in the Roman Senate. This compares to the Senate of the United States, which is comprised of 100 members. Romans came to be senators when they amassed fortunes and became favorites of the people through carefully managed public exposure. The second body of men controlling the affairs of Rome were the tribunes, who represented the issues and needs of various population sectors, just as the House of Representatives, with 435 members, deal with the issues and needs of the states they represent. Rome had a Constitution, just as the United States does, but the Roman Constitution prohibited senators from engaging in business. The United States Constitution has no such restriction, which is why both senators and representatives become extremely wealthy after they are elected. Election to the Congress is a sure path to wealth.

The third entity in Roman political life, the equites, were so named because members of this group originated among the cavalrymen: the horse soldiers. The equites engaged in a wide range of commercial enterprises, including banking, trading, and money lending. They converted booty from wars into cash. They obtained contracts for public works and collected taxes. They also engaged in secret deals with senators, which was illegal, but ignored.

Initially part of the same social group growing up, the senators, tribunes, and the equites chose separate paths to success. Some chose to follow money, and some chose to become soldiers. The equites were the finance-capital group of Roman life. The military men and their weapons makers became the military-industrial complex, exactly as it is in the United States.

In America, the military-industrial group has succeeded in gaining control of the United States government—and they manage the survival of the nation because of the *Pax Americana* that Marshall initiated. But alas, in a staggering decision by the Supreme Court in *Citizens United v. Federal Election Commission*, No. 08-205, 558 U.S. 310 (2010), the court allowed political donations to be made to election campaigns for House and Senate seats by nonprofit and for-profit organizations, corporations, labor unions—and *foreign countries*, whether they be friend or foe of the United States.

The finance-capital group somehow got control of the Supreme Court. They are challenging the military-industrial complex and the *Pax Americana* that keeps the nation safe.

President Obama contended, "Last week the Supreme Court reversed a century of law to open the floodgates for special interests—including foreign corporations, to spend without limit in our elections."[182]

In 2014, 13 House of Representatives campaigns were funded by at least $1 million in donations from unnamed donors, and in another 17 House seats such unnamed donors comprised half of the money the candidates spent to get elected. In addition, another $700 million was estimated to have been donated by unnamed groups interested in a particular candidate.[183]

Politicians are now for sale as never before in American history, and it is conceivable that radical Islamists and other enemies of the nation will quickly take advantage. Worse, these huge influxes of money from special interest groups, corporations, or individuals will overwhelm the ability of the American people to elect the person they deem best for the job.

Presidents clearly fall into one of two categories: they are either backed by the finance-capital group or they are backed by the military-industrial complex. President Barak Obama is an exception. Neither a military man nor a wealthy one, he is isolated from both. His reputation is flailed by the propaganda of the finance-capital group, and his military decisions are forced upon him by circumstances being managed by the military-industrial complex. With only The People to support him, a people increasingly propagandized to perceive him as a failure, he has nowhere to turn for validation.

As for the nation's history, the battle for control that is under way in America will turn the nation into an *Imperium*.

Today, the majority of potential voters in America sit back and do not vote because they have concerned themselves with things other than the men who rule them—just as the Roman people became content to let the Senate govern the expanding Empire. Roman citizens expected the Senate to manage the military, the Empire's finances, and foreign policy. The parallel between what happened in Rome and what is happening in the United States could not be clearer

As for who is in charge of wars, Congress obliged President Johnson by passing the Gulf of Tonkin Resolution in 1963, which provided Johnson with the exclusive right to use military force without consulting the Senate. Shortly after the World Trade towers were destroyed President Bush asserted that a president had the right to wage war without the approval of Congress, and the Congress granted him those emergency powers . . . in direct conflict with the Constitution. Those same emergency powers exist today. President Obama stated he could go to war without Congressional approval so long as a NATO nation was involved in the conflict. Congress has never challenged these exceptions to the Constitution because it makes the president completely responsible for all matters military and any wars that happen. This stance ensures their reelection from a public weary of war.

This circumstance could not be a closer parallel to what happened in Rome. Ultimately, the Roman tribunes, senators, and the equites stepped back from taking responsibility for any of the many wars Rome engaged in to protect her wealth, for to do so would have endangered the positive opinion of the people upon which their positions in Roman society were dependent.[184] Instead, they provided the Emperor with the power to do as he pleased.

Over time, the Roman senators and the tribunes ceased to represent the people and came to represent only themselves, just as is happening in the United States today with the Senate and the House of Representatives.

Another parallel can be made. When Caesar ushered in the realm of the Emperor, he was the first of a family-based succession to that role that existed for decades. Caesar was succeeded by Augustus, whom Caesar named as his adopted son and heir. The Kennedy family was prepared to begin the tradition of keeping the presidency in the family; the Bush family succeeded. With 12 years of Bush presidencies extant, yet another Bush is posited as the Republican nominee for the next election to that office. Keeping rulers in the family became the norm in Rome, and is in danger of becoming the norm in the United States.

Augustus, who succeeded Caesar, ruled with autocratic power over the Empire and was a military dictator. He established a new Constitution, and a period the relative peace ensued . . . known as the *Pax Romana* . . . which was characterized by continuing wars of expansion and control far from Rome, while peace and tranquility reigned in Rome itself. Similarly, the United States fights wars outside the United States to ensure the supply of oil, and one day those wars will ensure the supply of food, if not water.

The Islamists are and always will be a threat only to the supply of oil because they are geographically pinned down to the deserts of the Middle East. The United States can and will contain them in their deserts, just as Roman military leaders contained any threats to the Empire with military interventions, regardless of the distance from Rome.

Yet another parallel can be found. To the military mind, human life is an asset to be conserved for the ultimate purpose of war, and war is to be used as expeditiously as possible to achieve victory over threats to the homeland. In the closing days of World War II, Truman loosed an atomic bomb on Hiroshima (90,000 to 140,000 men, women, and children died), and just to make sure Japan got the message, 2 days later, he dropped another on Nagasaki (73,000 men, women, and children died). Both cities were completely destroyed by a single bomb each, regardless of civilians. In Roman wars, the cost in lives of winning was similarly irrelevant.

It was made abundantly clear that civilian deaths were observably irrelevant during World War II in Europe. At the end of the war, Munich, Dresden, Hamburg, and a dozen other German cities had been bombed flat. What was left were mounds of rubble, a mixture of what was left of houses, streets, historical buildings, furniture and paintings, family heirlooms, and records. Bodies and body parts of men, women, and children were all mixed together with the rubble, impossible to separate. There was neither manpower nor machines left to remove and identify the victims. As in other German cities, in Munich, all the rubble and bodies were scooped up and a mountain was made of it just outside the city, a cross on top. It is still there. Pilgrimages are made to visit the site, and flowers are laid at the cross. Underneath are entire families, civilians who got in the way.

In more recent times when the United States invaded Iraq, a change of strategy from World War II was observed: bombs were used to strike specific military targets rather than bomb cities and towns into oblivion. Yet, civilian men, women, and children still got in the way. Roman armies operated under a different military strategy. Civilians mattered not. Only winning mattered. And Rome never changed that strategy.

The key figure guiding the formation of the current philosophy of war in the United States, which is to win at all costs, was George Catlett Marshall. Unknowingly, we live under his spell in a world he created and guided into being, together with a handful of associates. As was said of Napoleon Bonaparte, Marshall, in the form of the *Pax Americana,* rules over us all: our nations and armies, our public opinion, our whole political existence, and all the more so the less we are conscious of it.

Now well established, the phenomenon he created has become the Form of a world that men of command have no option but to follow. There is no going back to the secondary role the United States had played on the global stage before World War II. The pacifistic United States has become covertly combative and intrinsically aggressive.

For almost a century, the American catchword has been "freedom"—for the world, for everyone. But the

American mode of freedom has contingent requirements that include such niceties as dealing with the World Bank, securing credits, providing materials internationally, buying "trade goods," purchasing arms, maintaining weapons and investing in new ones—in other words, a tiered integration with the force field of American economics and participation in the new "democratic"[185] America driven in part by the finance-capital group and in part by the military-industrial complex, at odds with each other. One will win.

The advent of the first emperor of the United States is not far ahead.

He will be called President.

The only major alternative to those who oppose the United States is to make a journey to Moscow for assistance, especially Third World countries. However, factually there is no Third World. There are only peripheral states of the two major powers, the United States and Russia, and it is only of incidental importance historically which camp an uncommitted so-called Third-World nation falls into.

The world since 1945, from the perspective of the conflict between big money and big military, is not a world confused by ideology, despairing hopes, or visionary dreams, but is a world of facts; hence, a world whose mechanics move at the behest of the great fact-men capable of dealing with the elements that are the hallmark of 21st-century Western civilization.

The United States is not a democracy. It is an oligarchy. The characteristics of an oligarchy are that power and control are held by a small number of people. These people are distinguished by any one of several factors such as wealth, family ties, royalty, religion, education, politics, or the military. Aristotle was the first to use the term *oligarchy* as a word for rule by the rich.

With the ultimate power to run the nation and conduct wars all but secure in the hands of whomever is president, and the executive powers the president has to start wars without the approval of lawmakers, the beginnings of the *Imperium* are secure. The doings in the House of Representatives and the Senate have become performance art only. The focus is on reelection, not on the ultimate destiny of the nation. That destiny is currently in the hands of the military-industrial complex, a self-sustaining phenomenon, and one that will react to any suggestion that the military budget or size be reduced. Even talking about reducing the military budget can have catastrophic consequences for those who have the temerity to suggest it. Presidents and others who threaten to reduce the military do so at their peril.

> *The moving finger writes, and, having writ,*
> *Moves on: nor all thy Piety nor Wit*
> *Shall lure it back to cancel half a line,*
> *Nor all thy tears wash out a Word of it.*
> Omar Khayyam, The Rubaiyat, 1872

The story of America has yet to come to its final disposition. As to what will happen next, it will not happen tomorrow, it will not happen next year, it will not happen in a decade, but it will happen. The harbingers of the end are there now for the observant to see. For instance, Mitt Romney's remark that 47% of Americans "are dependent upon government, who believe that they are victims, who believe the government has a responsibility to care for them, who believe that they are entitled to health care, to food, to housing, to you-name-it" was a clear statement of the attitude of the oligarchs, those 100 men who own two-thirds of the wealth in the nation, about the people of America. And the people arose in reaction to that remark and elected Barak Obama by a wide margin. To the observant, the Romney remark rings of Marie Antoinette's sneer about the French citizenry, "Let them eat cake," which she said at a time when the economy of France was in a shambles and the people were starving. And the people arose and chopped off her head and the heads of every other member of the ruling class they could find.

The oligarchs in America have the same attitude toward the citizenry that the aristocracy of France had toward their citizens, and in the end, the people will arise one day and chop off their heads. The Supreme Court ruling allowing money from foreign governments to fund political campaigns in the United States will result in candidates winning elections when they have a "47%" attitude toward the people they are supposed to represent, or worse, reflect the views of oligarchs or foreign nations. The citizenry *will* notice.

Another harbinger of the disposition to come, and one that supports the hypothesis above, is the first small stirrings of anarchy on the streets of America as people begin to rise up against those who rule them. As history shows, the oligarchs turn to the military to protect them. The beginnings of that turn can already be seen as local police departments are beginning to be pushed from Washington to arm themselves with military style equipment and request the assistance of the military when they can no longer control the anarchy. Today's anarchists target one cause, racial inequality, but causes change, and grow more encompassing, and as the representatives and senators in Washington increasingly represent those who fund their political campaigns instead of the people, anarchy will arise and challenge the very foundations upon which America was founded.

Another parallel to what will become the fate of America is found in Roman history. When Rome was engaged in defending itself from outside forces, it was also struggling with severe financial problems as a result of constant war, overspending, crippling taxes, and the rich becoming richer and the poor becoming poorer, as is happening in the United States today.

As the cost of maintaining Rome's military skyrocketed, the nation's infrastructure fell into a state of decay. America's infrastructure is vastly in need of repair, but it is not happening because of the need to fund continuing wars. Roman politicians engaged in an array of practices to serve their own interests, not the interests of the people, and the Roman Senate failed to act to stop it because of their own internal corruption and incompetence. As a result, the people lost all trust in the government and the form of the country was overthrown and an *Imperium* ensued.

The same drift into a new Form of the United States is evident.

We live in an era of a "do nothing" Congress that fails to represent the people and have abdicated their role to wage war to the executive branch . . . the branch most vulnerable to the finance-capital group.

The finance-capital group seeks only money. Their goal is not a long-lasting Union, or an America, bold and free. Their view of the world is global and they possess no allegiance to the soil of the United States. No legislation will be allowed to stand in their way, no will of the people will stop them, no aspect of life will be free of their influence. They deal entirely with thought, and penetrate every aspect of life . . . farming, industry, science, labor, art, education, government . . . all of that which is encompassed within the concept of the United States of America. But eventually the finance-capital group, as is shown by history, "fades out as soon as it has thought its economic world to finality."[186] At the moment when money is celebrating its final victories, anarchy will bring it down, and the military-industrial complex, rooted in the soil and comprised of form and substance, will be the salvation of the nation in an altered Form. The end game of Marshall's *Pax Americana* will come to pass, *other men will come*, and the resulting Form of the nation, as in Rome, will prevail for a thousand years.

BIBLIOGRAPHY

Acheson, D. (1960). *Present at the Creation: My Years in the State Department*. New York, NY: Norton.

Acheson, D. (1961). *Sketches From Life of Men I Have Known*. New York, NY: Harper.

Argo, R. A. (1997). *Force XXI: Precision Engagement: The Need for a Joint Force Coordinator*. Fort Leavenworth, KS: U.S Army Command and General Staff College, School of Advanced Military Studies.

Ambrose, S. E. (1983). *Eisenhower: 1890–1952*. New York, NY: Simon & Schuster.

Bemis, S. F. (Ed.). (1927). *American Secretaries of State and Their Diplomacy, Vols. 1–16*. New York, NY: Knopf.

Bishop, J. (1975). *FDR's Last Year: April 1944–April 1945*. New York, NY: Pocket Books.

Black, C. (2007). *Richard M. Nixon: A Life in Full*. New York, NY: Simon & Schuster.

Black, J. (2003). *World War Two: A Military History*. New York, NY: Psychology Press.

Bogart, G., & Kellogg, V. L. (1916).*Losses of Life in Modern Wars, Austria-Hungary: France* (H. Westergaard, Ed.). New York, NY: Clarendon Press.

Bouscaren, A. T. (1965). *Last of the Mandarins: Diem of Vietnam*. Pittsburg, PA: DuQuesne University Press.

Bowies, R. R., & Immerman, R. H. (1998).*Waging Peace: How Eisenhower Shaped an Enduring Cold War Strategy*. New York, NY: Oxford University Press.

Bresnahan, T., Gambardella, A., & Saxenian, A. (2001). Old Economy Inputs for New Economy Outcomes: Cluster Formation in the New Silicon Valleys.*Industrial and Corporate Change, 10,* 835–860.http://dx.doi.org/10.1093/icc/10.4.835

Bruce, J. W., & Wilcox, C. (Eds.). (1998). *The Changing Politics of Gun Control*. Lanham, MD: Rowman & Littlefield.

Burgan, M. (2011).*Ronald Reagan*. New York, NY: DK.

Burnes, B. (2003). *Harry S. Truman: His Life and Times*. Kansas City, MO: Star Books.

Cannon, J. (with Cannon, S.). (2013). *Gerald R. Ford: An Honorable Life*. Ann Arbor, MI: University of Michigan Press.

Carlyle, T. (2002).*The French Revolution: A History*. New York, NY: Modern Library. (Original work published 1837)

Caro, R. A. (2013). *The Years of Lyndon Johnson: Vol. 4, The Passage of Power*. New York, NY: Bodley Head.

Churchill, W. L. S. (2011). *The Second World War*. New York, NY: Random House. (Original work published 1948)

Cole, B. D. (1972). *United States Treaty Commitments in Southern Asia, 1950-1954*. Monterey, CA: Archives of the Naval Postgraduate School.

Conetta, C. (2003). Appendix 2: Iraqi Combatant and Noncombatant Fatalities in the 1991 Gulf War. In *The Wages of War: Iraqi Combatant and Noncombatant Fatalities in the 2003 Conflict*. Cambridge, MA: Project on Defense Alternatives.

Cox, P. (2014).*John Nance Garner on the Vice Presidency— In Search of the Proverbial Bucket*. Austin: University of Texas, Briscoe Center for American History.

Cushman, J. H., Jr., Kirkpatrick, D. D., & Schmitt, E. (2010, January 28).Taking a Closer Look at Assertions on Domestic and Foreign Policy. *The New York Times*. Retrieved from http://www.nytimes.com

Dallek, R. (2003). *An Unfinished Life: John F. Kennedy, 1917-1963*. Boston, MA: Little, Brown.

Dallek, R. (2007). *Nixon and Kissinger: Partners in Power*. New York, NY: Harper Collins.

Dallek, R. (2008). *Harry S. Truman: The American Presidents Series: The 33rd President, 1945-1953*. New York, NY: Macmillan.

Davis, J. H. (1984). *The Kennedys: Dynasty and Disaster, 1848–1983*. New York, NY: McGraw-Hill.

Diem, B. (with Chanoff, D.). (1999). *In the Jaws of History*. Bloomington: Indiana University Press. (Original work published 1942)

Eisenhower, D. D. (1961, January 17).*Farewell Address*. Retrieved from http://www.Americanrhetoric.com/speeches/dwightdeisenhowerfarewell.html

Ferrell, R. H. (1994). *Harry S. Truman: A Life*. Columbia: University of Missouri Press.

Gayed, J. (2008, March 4). *A Nation of Riflemen First Needs Men*. Free Republic. Retrieved from http://www. freerepublic.com/focus/news/2038359/posts

Gettleman, M. E. (Ed.). (1966). *Vietnam: History, Documents, and Opinions on a Major World Crisis*. New York, NY: Penguin Books.

Ginor, I. (2000, June 10). How the Six-Day War Almost Led to Armageddon. *The Guardian (London)*.Retrieved from http://www.theguardian.com/

Goethe, J. W. v. (2007). *Wisdom and Experience*. New York, NY: Read Books. (Original work published 1949)

Gold, M. (2014, November 28). Groups Funded by Secret Donors Buffeted Two Dozen House Races in 2014. *The Washington Post*. Retrieved from http://www. washingtonpost.com

Green, J. R. (2000). *The Presidency of George Busy (American Presidency Series)*. Lawrence: University Press of Kansas.

Haass, R. N. (2005, Fall). *The Case for "Integration."* Washington, DC: Council on Foreign Relations.

Halberstam, D. (2008). *The Coldest Winter: America and the Korean War*. New York, NY: Macmillan.

Hoffman, D. (1989, December 4). Bush and Gorbachev Hail New Cooperation. *The Washington Post*. Retrieved from http://www.washingtonpost.com

Hogan, M. J. (1998). *A Cross of Iron: Harry S. Truman and the Origins of the National Security State, 1945-1954*. New York, NY: Cambridge University Press

Holmes, R., Strachan, H., & Bellamy, C. (Eds.).(2001).*The Oxford Companion to Military History*. New York, NY: Oxford University Press.

Homeland Security Act of 2002, Pub. L. No. 113-164, 128 Stat. 1867 (2014).

Hybel, A. R.,& Kaufman, J.M. (2006). *The Bush Administration and Saddam Hussein: Deciding on Conflict*. New York, NY: Palgrave Macmillan.

Issacson, W. (2005).*Kissinger: A Biography*. New York, NY: Simon & Schuster. (Original work published 1992).

Jacobs. S. (2006).*Cold War Mandarin: Ngo Dinh Diem and the Origins of America's War in Vietnam, 1950–1963*. Lanham, MD: Rowan & Littlefield.

Kates, D. B., Jr., Schaffer, H. E., Lattimer, J. K., Murray, G. B., & Cassem, E. H. (1995). Bad Medicine: Doctors and Guns. In D. Kopel (Ed.), *Guns: Who Should Have Them*(pp. 233–308). Amherst, NY: Prometheus Books.

Kaufman, B. I., & Kaufman, S. (1993). *The Presidency of James Earl Carter, Jr.* Lawrence: University Press of Kansas.

KirKendall, R. S. (Ed.). (1989). *The Harry S. Truman Encyclopedia*. Boston, MA: G. K. Hall.

Kissinger, H. (1954).*Peace, Legitimacy, and the Equilibrium: A Study of the Statesmanship of Castlereagh and Metternich*. Cambridge, MA: Author.

Kohls, G. G. (2014, January 19). MLK's Warning of America's Spiritual Death. *Consortium News*. Retrieved from http://consortiumnews.com/2014/01/19/mlks-warning-of-americas-spiritual-death/

Kurland, G. (1972). *Lyndon Baines Johnson: President Caught in an Ordeal of Power*. Charlotteville, NY: SamHar Press.

Lansford, T. (2001). *The Lords of Foggy Bottom: American Secretaries of State and the World They Shaped*. Baldwin Place, NY: Encyclopedia Society.

Leckie, G. P. (1962). *Conflict: The History of the Korean War 1950–53*. New York, NY: Putnam.

Lundberg, F. (2008).*America's 60 Families*. New York, NY: Vanguard Press. (Original work published 1937)

Lyons, M. J. (1994).*World War I: A Short History*. New York, NY: Prentice Hall.

Maneli, M. (1975, January 27). Vietnam: '63 and Now. *The New York Times*. Retrieved from http://www.nytimes.com

Maraniss, D. (1996). *First in His Class: A Biography of Bill Clinton*. New York, NY: Simon & Schuster.

Marshall, K. T., Bland, L. I., & Stevens, S. R. (Eds.). (2003). *The papers of George Catlett Marshall*. Baltimore, MD: Johns Hopkins University Press.

Marchetti, V., & Marks, J. D. (1974).*The CIA and the Cult of Intelligence*. New York, NY: Knopf.

Martin, B. K. (2004). *Under the Loving Care of the Fatherly Leader: North Korea and the Kim Dynasty*. New York, NY: Macmillan.

McCullough, D. (1992). *Truman*. New York, NY: Simon & Schuster.

McNichol, D. (2006). *The Roads that Built America: The Incredible Story of the U.S. Interstate System*. New York, NY: Sterling Press.

Meyer, G. J. (2007). *A World Undone: The Story of the Great War 1914 to 1918*. New York, NY: Random House.

Mihalkanin, E. S. (2004). *America Statesmen: Secretaries of State from John Jay to Colin Powell*. New York, NY: Greenwood Press.

Moorhead, M. (2012, September 18).Mitt Romney Says 47% of Americans Pay No Income Tax. *The Tampa Bay Times*. Retrieved from http://www.tampabay.com

Myers, G. (1937). *History of the Great American Fortunes*. New York, NY: Random House.

Napier, R., & Gershenfeld, M. K. (1993).*Groups, Theory, and Experience* (7thed.). Boston, MA: Houghton Mifflin.

Nelson, J.,& Clift, E. (1986, April 15). U.S. Retaliates, Bombs Libya: Terror-Related Sites Hit in Response to Berlin Conflict. *The Los Angeles Times*.

Niiler, E. (2014, November 17). NASA Builds a Time-Machine Telescope 100 Times as Powerful as the Hubble. *The Washington Post*. Retrieved from http://www.washingtonpost.com

O'Brien, M. (2005).*John F. Kennedy: A Biography*. New York, NY: Macmillan.

O'Donnell, K. (1970). LBJ and the Kennedys [Book excerpt]. *Life Magazine, 69*(6), 51–52.Retrieved from http://www.life.com

Patterson, J. T. (1996). *Grand Expectations: The History of the United States, 1945–1974*. New York, NY: Oxford University Press.

Pax Romana. (2003). Chicago, IL: Encyclopedia Britannica.

Plumer, B. (2013, January 7). America's Staggering Defense Budget, in Charts. *The Washington Post*. Retrieved from http://www.washingtonpost.com

Porter, M. E. (1998). Clusters and the New Economies of Competition. *Harvard Business Review, 76*(6), 77–90. Retrieved from https://hbr.org

Raskin, M. G. (1965).*The Vietnam Reader: Articles and Documents of American Foreign Policy and the Vietnam Crisis*. New York NY: Vintage Books.

Raymond, E. (2006). *From my Cold, Dead Hands: Charlton Heston and American Politics*. Lexington, KY: University Press of Kentucky.

Reagan, R. (1988). Public Papers of the Presidents of the United States: The Administration of Ronald Reagan. Washington, DC

Rhodes, R. (1988). Epidemic of War Deaths; Statistics on War-Related Deaths Through History. *Science News, 134*(8), 124.Retrieved from https://www.sciencenews.org

Rowan, R. W. (1934).Spies and the Next War. New York, NY: Robert M. McBride & Company.

Rugaber, C. S., & Boak, J. (2014, January 27). *Wealth Gap: A Guide to What it is, Why it Matters*. Washington, DC: AP News.

Saxenian, A. (1994). *Regional Advantage: Cluster and Competition in Silicon Valley and Route 128*. Cambridge, MA: Harvard University Press.

Scullard, H. H. (1963). *From the Gracchi to Nero: A history of Rome from 133 B.C. to AD 68*.New York, NY: Methuen.

Setz-Wald, A. (2011, May 2). Flashback: Bush on Bin Laden: 'I really just don't spend that much time on him' [Web log]. *ThinkProgress*. Retrieved from http://thinkprogress.org/person/alex-seitz-wald/page/76/

Smith, J. E. (2007). *FDR*. New York, NY: Random House

Smith, J. E. (2012). *Eisenhower: In War and Peace*. New York, NY: Random House.

Smith, W. B. (1950). *My 3 Years in Moscow*. Philadelphia, PA: Lippincott.

Solzhenitsyn, A. I. (1974). *Letter to the Soviet Leaders*. New York, NY: Collins.

Spengler, O. (1928). *The Decline of the West (Vol. II)*.New York, NY: Knopf

Spitzer, R. J. (1995).*The Politics of Gun Control*. New York, NY: Chatham House.

Steinberg, A. (1968). *Sam Johnson's Boy: Closeup of the President from Texas*. New York, NY: Macmillan.

Stimson, H. L. (2007). His diary, November 6, 1942.In H. L Stimson & M. Bundy (Eds), *On Active Service in Peace and War*. New York, NY: Read Books.

The New York Times. (1991, February 28). War in the gulf: Commander's briefing; Schwarzkopf news conference on Gulf war. New York, NY: The Times.

Thompson, J. (1968). *Six Seconds in Dallas: A Micro-Study of the Kennedy Assassination*. New York, NY: B. Geis.

Trask, R. R. (1985). *The Secretaries of Defense: A Brief History, 1947–1985*.Washington, DC: U.S. Department of Defense

United States Policy in the Korean War.(1950, July 20). *The New York Times.* Retrieved from http://www.nytimes.com

Universal Military Training: Hearings Before the Committee on Armed Services, United States Senate, 18th Cong. 2 (Testimony of George C. Marshall).

Vandiver, F.E. (1977). *Black Jack: The Life and Times of John. J. Pershing, Vol. 1.* College Station, TX: Texas A&M University Press.

Von Bertalanffy, L. (1968). *General System Theory: Essays on its Foundation and Development* (rev. ed.). New York, NY: Basic Books.

"War in the Gulf Commander's Briefing; Excerpts from Schwarzkopf News Conference." (1991, February 28). *The New York Times.* Retrieved from http://www.nytimes.com

Weber, E. (1989). *The Western Tradition*[Lecture Series]. Los Angeles: University of California at Los Angeles.

Weinberg, G. L. (1994). *A World at Arms: A Global History of World War II.* New York, NY: Cambridge University Press.

Weingroff, R. F. (1996). *Federal-Aid Highway Act of 1956: Creating the Interstate System.* Washington, DC: Federal Highway Administration.

Wheeler, E. J., Funk, I. K., & Woods, W. S. (Eds.).(1906, January-June).Killing Women and Children in Jolo. *The Literary Digest* (Vol. 32, pp. 433–434).

Whelan, R. (1990). *Drawing the Line: The Korean War.* Boston, MA: Little, Brown.

White, M. (2011). *Source List and Detailed Death Tolls for the Primary Megadeaths of the Twentieth Century*. Retrieved from http://necrometrics.com/20c5m.htm

The White House, Office of Management & Budget. (2014). *Department of Defense Budget*. Washington, DC: Author.

Winters, J. (2011).*Oligarchy*. New York, NY: Cambridge University Press.

ENDNOTES

[1]M. J. Lyons, *World War I: A Short History* (New York: Prentice Hall, 1994).

[2]J. Black, *World War II: A Military History* (New York: Routledge, 2003).

[3]G. Bogart & V. L. Kellogg, *Losses of Life in Modern Wars, Austria-Hungary: France* (New York: Clarendon Press, 1916).

[4]H. H. Scullard, *From the Gracchi to Nero* (New York: Methuen, 1963).

[5]G. L. Weinberg, *A World at Arms: A Global History of World War II* (New York: Cambridge University Press, 1994).

[6]J. Bishop, *FDR's Last Year* (New York: Pocket Books, 1975).

[7]Bishop, 1975.

[8]D. McCullough, *Truman* (New York: Simon & Schuster, 1992).

[9]McCullough, 1992.

[10]Bishop, 1975.

[11]J. E. Smith, *FDR* (New York: Random House, 2007).

[12]Bishop, 1975.

[13]Bishop, 1975.

[14]Bishop, 1975.

[15]Reagan, *Public Papers of the Presidents of the United States*, 61.

[16]G. Myers, *History of the Great American Fortunes* (New York: Random House, 1937).

[17]F. Lundberg, *America's 60 Families* (New York: Vanguard Press, 2008).

[18]O. Spengler, *Decline of the West, Vol. II* (New York: Important Books, 2013).

[19]C. S. Rugaber & J. Boak, *Wealth Gap: A Guide to What it is, Why it Matters* (AP News, 2014).

[20]J. Winters, *Oligarchy* (New York: Cambridge University Press, 2011).

[21]In January 1946, President Harry Truman created the Central Intelligence Group, which was the direct precursor to the Central Intelligence Agency. The original mission was to gather information about individuals, organizations, and foreign governments, not to assist the Armed Forces, which had their own intelligence services, but to support the members of Congress. The famous "covert" operations were introduced well afterward.

[22]Activity of this kind has nothing to do with Karl Marx and the world he structured for purposes of revolution. Marx was a professional revolutionist. He saw the world from below, by design, adopting the perspective of his concept, "proletariat." Proletariat is a counter concept of Marx's "Capitalist." His was an outlook, not an overlook. The objective of that which he created was and always

has been to subvert and to overthrow the West and her ways.

[23]T. Carlyle, *The French Revolution: A History* (New York: Modern Library, 2002), 14.

[24]F. E. Vandiver, *Black Jack: The Life and Times of John. J. Pershing* (City: Texas A&M University Press, 1977).

[25]Vandiver, 1977.

[26]E. J. Wheeler, I. K. Funk, & W. S. Woods, *The Literary Digest* (New York: Funk & Wagnalls, 1906).

[27]Vandiver, 1977.

[28]G. J. Meyer, *A World Undone: The Story of the Great War 1914 to 1918*(New York: Random House, 2007).

[29]Note: Coincidentally, the length of Rome's Third Carthaginian War almost 2000 years earlier in a similar period of continuing wars.

[30]J. E. Smith, 2007.

[31]J. T. Patterson, *Grand Expectations: The History of the United States, 1945–1974* (New York: Oxford University Press, 1996).

[32]W. B Smith, *My Three Years in Moscow* (Philadelphia: Lippincott, 1950).

[33]W. B. Smith, 1950, 322.

[34]A. I. Solzhenitsyn, *Letter to the Soviet Leaders* (New York: Collins, 1974), 15.

[35]K. T. Marshall, L.T. B, & S. R. Stevens, *The Papers of George Catlett Marshall* (New York: Johns Hopkins University Press, 2003).

[36]S. F. Bemis, *American Secretaries of State and Their Diplomacy* (New York: Knopf, 1927), 15: 27.

[37]D. Acheson, *Sketches from Life of Men I Have Known* (New York: Harper, 1961), 150-151.

[38]Acheson, 1961, 150-151,

[39]Acheson, 1961, 150-151.

[40]D. Acheson, *Present at the Creation* (New York: Norton, 1960).

[41]Bemis, 1927, 15: 16.

[42]J. W. Goethe, "Maxims and Reflections," in *Goethe: Wisdom and Experience* (New York: Read Books, 2007), 517.

[43]Bemis, 1927, 16: 28.

[44]Bemis, 1927, 16: 28.

[45]Bemis, 1927, 16: 28.

[46]Acheson, 1961, 15, 53, 124.

[47]The first part of this book is about Marshall and the Americans and their politics since 1945, not about the Soviet Union, except as the decisive polarity factor on the world scene from World War II to the present day. The key, and the heartland, of what was called the "Soviet Union" for over three generations is Great Russia.

The stamp of Great Russia is to be found everywhere. About two thirds of the area and the population of the Soviet Union is Great Russian and is more or less included within the borders of the great state known as the R.F.S.F.R. This is the homeland of the real Russians. These are the people whom Stalin toasted "first of all" at the great Kremlin victory banquet on May 25, 1945, when he referred to them as "the most outstanding of all the nationalities forming part of the Soviet Union."Despite disclaimers and dissimulation, Russia's policy today is a continuation of Great Russian expansion that periodically and persistently threatens the West.

[48]Bemis, 15: 53–54.

[49]W. B. Smith, 1950.

[50]Bemis, 15: 74–75. Marshall's approval of the president's speech is from *American Secretaries of State*, 74–75.

[Soviet Communism is a] "subtle, powerful instrument of Russian imperialism" The preceding quote is from p. 356 of Acheson's "Present at the Creation." The rest of the paragraph is from W.B. Smith's "My three years in Moscow."

[51]Bemis, 1927, 15: 75.

[52]Note: Sources for this and the following are from (a) United States Policy in the Korean War, U.S. Department of State Publication, Far Eastern Series 34, July 20, 1950; (b) *New York Times*, June 26, 27, 28, 1950.

[53]Bemis, 1927, 15.

[54]This quote is from Marshall's testimony before the Senate Armed Forces Committee in March 1948.

[55]M. J. Hogan. *A Cross of Iron: Harry S. Truman and the Origins of the National Security State, 1945-1954*(New York: Cambridge University Press, 1998).

[56]D. Halberstam, *The Coldest Winter: America and the Korean War* (New York: Macmillan, 2008).

[57]Halberstam, 2008.

[58]B. D. Cole, *United States Treaty Commitments in Southern Asia, 1950-1954* (Archives of the Naval Postgraduate School, 1972).

[59]B. Martin, *Under the Loving Care of the Fatherly Leader: North Korea and the Kim Dynasty* (New York: Macmillan,2004).

[60]G.P. Leckie, *Conflict: The History of the Korean War 1950-1953* (New York: Putnam, 1962), 13–17.

[61]However, in spite of all this, paraphrasing the words of Winston Churchill, "Democracy is an awful way to govern people, but it's the best thing we've got going."

[62]R. R. Trask, *The Secretaries of Defense: A Brief History, 1947–1985* (Washington, DC: U.S. Department of Defense, 1985).

[63]Note: The mid-19th century saw the introduction of the newly developed railroads as a weapon of war during the American Civil War. For the first time, vast numbers of soldiers, artillery, and other support hardware could be moved from one battleground to another with unheard of speed. It was this same factor, and in the same period, that finally permitted Germany the possibility of fighting a two-front war simultaneously on her eastern and western borders, thus moving her overnight into the ranks of the major powers.

[64]M.G. Raskin, *The Vietnam Reader: Articles and Documents of American Foreign Policy and the Vietnam Crisis* (New York: Vintage Books, 1965), 377–402.

[65]Halberstam, 2008.

[66]Halberstam, 2008.

[67]Leckie, 1962.

[68]Office of the Historian, *Biographies of the Secretaries of State* (n.d.). Note: While always in the background, ever watchful, stands the Soviet Union; ready at a moment's

notice for an opportunity to move onstage to fulfill a modern day-Hyksos role.

[69]E.S. Mihalkanin, *American Statesmen: Secretaries of State from John Jay to Colin Powell* (New York: Greenwood Press, 2004).

[70]Office of the Historian (n.d.): George Catlett Marshall.

[71]Raskin, 1965, 377–402.

[72]S. Jacobs, *Cold War Mandarin: Ngo Dinh Diem and the Origins of America's War in Vietnam, 1950-1963.* (Lanham: Rowan & Littlefield, 2006).

[73]B. Diem, *In the Jaws of History* (Bloomington: Indiana University Press, 1999).

[74]Diem, 1999.

[75]Diem, 1999.

[76]Diem, 1999.

[77]Diem, 1999.

[78]S. F. Ambrose, *Eisenhower: 1890–1952* (New York: Simon & Schuster, 1983).

[79]Ambrose, 1983.

[80]Ambrose, 1983, 38.

[81]J. H. Davis, *The Kennedys: Dynasty & Disaster, 1848–1983* (New York, McGraw Hill,1984), 4.

[82]Davis, 1984, 44.

[83]Diem, 1999.

[84]Davis, 1984, 604.

[85]Diem, 1999.

[86]Diem, 1999, 105.

[87]Diem, 1999, 123.

[88]Diem, 1999, 123.

[89]Diem, 1999, 125.

[90]A. Steinberg, *Sam Johnson's Boy: Close up of the President from Texas* (New York: Macmillan, 1968).

[91]G. Kurland, *Lyndon Baines Johnson: President Caught in an Ordeal of Power* (Charlotteville: SamHar Press, 1972), 12–13.

[92]Kurland, 1972, 125.

[93]P. Cox, *John Nance Garner on the Vice Presidency—In Search of the Proverbial Bucket* (Austin: University of Texas, 2014).

[94]K. O'Donnell, "L.B.J. and the Kennedys" [Book excerpt], *Life Magazine* 69(1970): 51.

[95]O'Donnell, 1970, 51.

[96]O'Donnell, 1970, 51.

[97]Marshall said this in testimony to the Senate Armed Forces Committee in March 1948.

[98]M. O'Brien, *John F. Kennedy: A Biography* (New York: Macmillan, 2005).

[99]V. Marchetti& J. D. Marks, *The CIA and the Cult of Intelligence* (New York: Knopf, 1974), 29–30.

[100]Marchetti & Marks, 1974.

[101]J. Thompson, *Six Seconds in Dallas: A Micro-Study of the Kennedy Assassination* (New York: B. Geis, 1968).

[102]Since 1700, over 100 million people have been killed in war . . . 90% in the 20th century (R. Rhodes, "Epidemic of War Deaths; Statistics on War-Related Deaths Through History," *Science News* 134 (1988): 124.

[103]G. G. Kohls, "MLK's Warning of America's Spiritual Death," *Consortium News* (2014).

[104]B. Burnes, *Harry S. Truman: His Life and Times* (Kansas City: Star Books, 2003).

[105]R. Dallek, *Harry S. Truman: The American Presidents Series: The 33rd President, 1945–1953* (New York: Macmillan, 2008).

[106]R.S. KirKendall, *The Harry S Truman Encyclopedia* (Boston: G.K. Hall, 1989).

[107]R.H. Ferrell, *Harry S. Truman: A Life* (Columbia, University of Missouri Press, 1994).

[108]B. Plumer, "America's Staggering Defense Budget, in Charts," *The Washington Post,* January 7, 2013.

[109]The White House, Office of Management and Budget, *Department of Defense Budget* (2014).

[110]Ambrose, 1983.

[111]J. E. Smith: *Eisenhower in War and Peace* (New York: Random House, 2012).

[112]R. R. Bowies & R. H. Immerman, *Waging Peace: How Eisenhower Shaped an Enduring Cold War Strategy* (New York: Oxford University Press, 1998).

[113]D. McNichol, *The Roads that Built America: The Incredible Story of the U.S. Interstate System* (New York: Sterling Press, 2006).

[114]Plumer, 2013.

[115]M. O'Brien, 2005.

[116]M. O'Brien, 2005.

[117]R. Dallek, *An Unfinished Life: John F. Kennedy, 1917–1963* (Boston: Little, Brown, 2003).

[118]R. Dallek, 2003.

[119]Plumer, 2013.

[120] Plumer, 2013.

[121] R. A. Caro, *The Passage of Power: The Years of Lyndon Johnson: Vol. 4, The Passage of Power* (New York: Bodley Head, 2013).

[122] Caro, 2013.

[123] I. Ginor, "How the Six Day War Almost Led to Armageddon," *The Guardian* (2000).

[124] Plumer, 2013.

[125] C. Black, *Richard M. Nixon: A Life in Full* (New York: Simon & Schuster, 2007).

[126] W. Issacson, *Kissinger: A Biography* (New York: Simon &Schuster, 2005).

[127] Issacson, 2005.

[128] R. Dallek, *Nixon and Kissinger: Partners in Power* (New York: Harper Collins, 2007).

[129] Plumer, 2013.

[130] J. Cannon, *Gerald R. Ford: An Honorable Life* (Ann Arbor: University of Michigan Press, 2013).

[131] Cannon, 2013.

[132] Plumer, 2013.

[133] B. I. Kaufman & S. Kaufman, *The Presidency of James Earl Carter, Jr.* (Lawrence: University Press of Kansas, 1993).

[134] Kaufman& Kaufman, 1993.

[135] Plumer, 2013.

[136] M. Burgan, *Ronald Reagan* (New York: DK, 2011).

[137] Burgan, 2011.

[138] J. Nelson & E. Clift, "U.S. Retaliates, Bombs Libya: Terror-Related Sites Hit in Response to Berlin Conflict," *The Los Angeles Times*, April 15, 1986.

[139]Plumer, 2013.

[140]J. R. Green, *The Presidency of George Bush* (Lawrence: University Press of Kansas, 2000).

[141]Green, 2000.

[142]D. Hoffman, "Bush and Gorbachev Hail New Cooperation," *The Washington Post*, December 4, 1989.

[143]"War in the Gulf Commander's Briefing; Excerpts from Schwarzkopf News Conference," *The New York Times*, February 28, 1991.

[144]R. A. Argo, *Force XXI Precision Engagement: The Need for a Joint Force Coordinator* (Fort Leavenworth: U.S. Army Command and Control General Staff College, 1997).

[145]C. Conetta, *The Wages of War: Iraqi Combatant and Noncombatant Fatalities in the 1991 Gulf War* (Cambridge, MA: Project on Defense Alternatives, 2003).

[146]R. N. Haass, *The Case for "Integration"* (Washington, DC: Council of Foreign Relations, 2005).

[147]A. R. Hybel& J. M. Kaufmann, *The Bush Administration and Saddam Hussein: Deciding on Conflict* (New York: Palgrave MacMillan, 2006).

[148]Plumer, 2013.

[149]D. Maraniss, *First in His Class: A Biography of Bill Clinton* (New York: Simon & Schuster, 1996).

[150]Plumer, 2013.

[151]A. Setz-Wald, Flashback: Bush on Bin Laden: 'I Really Just Don't Spend That Much Time on Him' [Web log], *ThinkProgress*, May 2, 2011.

[152]Setz-Wald, 2011.

[153]Plumer, 2013

[154]M. Moorhead, "Mitt Romney Says 47 Percent of Americans Pay No Income Tax," *The Tampa Bay Times*, September 18, 2012.

[155]Plumer, 2013.

[156]*Encyclopedia Britannica*, 2003.

[157]*Encyclopedia Britannica*, 2003.

[158]R. C. Weingroff, *Federal-aid Highway Act of 1956: Creating the Interstate System* (Washington, DC: Federal Highway Administration, 1996).

[159]H. Kissinger, *Peace, Legitimacy, and the Equilibrium: A Study of the Statesmanship of Castlereagh and Metternich* (Cambridge: Author, 1954), 6.

[160]T. Bresnahan, A. Gambardella, & A. Saxenian, "Old Economy Inputs for New Economy Outcomes: Cluster Formation in the New Silicon Valleys," *Industrial and Corporate Change* 10 (2001): 835–860.

[161]M. E. Porter, "Clusters and the New Economics of Competition," *Harvard Business Review* 76 (1998): 77–90.

[162]A. Saxenian, *Regional Advantage: Cluster and Competition in Silicon Valley and Route 128* (Cambridge: Harvard University Press, 1994).

[163]Homeland Security Act of 2002 (2014).

[164]J. Gayed, A Nation of Riflemen First Needs Men, 2008.

[165]E. Raymond, *From My Cold, Dead Hands: Charlton Heston and American Politics*(Lexington: University Press of Kentucky, 2006).

[166]R. J. Spitzer, *The Politics of Gun Control*(New York: Chatham House, 1995).

[167] J. W. Bruce &C. Wilcox, *The Changing Politics of Gun Control* (Lanham: Rowman & Littlefield, 1998).

[168] D. B. Kates, Jr., H. E. Schaffer, J. K. Lattimer, G. B. Murray, & E. H. Cassem, "Bad Medicine: Doctors and Guns," in D. Kopel (Ed.), *Guns: Who Should Have Them* (Amherst: Prometheus Books, 1995), 233–308.

[169] Niiler, E., "NASA Builds a Time-Machine Telescope 100 Times as Powerful as the Hubble," *The Washington Post*, November 17, 2014.

[170] Supreme Court Decision, 1978.

[171] Sun Tzu, *The Art of War*, 4thcentury B.C.

[172] Rowan, 4.

[173] The Constitution of the United States of America.

[174] R. Napier & M. K. Gershenfeld, *Groups, Theory, & Experience* (Boston: Houghton Mifflin, 1993).

[175] L. von Bertalanffy, *General System Theory: Essays on its Foundation and Development* (New York: Basic Books, 1968).

[176] Napier & Gershenfeld, 1993.

[177] Von Bertalanffy, 1968.

[178] Von Bertalanffy, 1968.

[179] Kissinger, 1954, 7.

[180] R. Rhodes, "Epidemic of War Deaths; Statistics on War-Related Deaths Through History," *Science News* 134 (1988), 124.

[181] Von Bertalanffy, 1968.

[182] J. H. Cushman, Jr., D. D. Kirkpatrick, &E. Schmitt, "Taking a Closer Look at Assertions on Domestic and Foreign Policy," *New York Times*, January 28, 2010.

[183]M. Gold, "Groups Funded by Secret Donors Buffeted Two Dozen House Races in 2014,"*The Washington Post,* November 28, 2014.

[184]Gold, 2014, 6

[185]Gold, 2014, 6

[186]Spengler, 1928, 506

Made in the USA
San Bernardino, CA
10 February 2015